A CONSUMING PASSION

Inspired recipes from *Le Gavroche to Zibibbo*

ADAM NEWELL

Photographs by Murray Lloyd

Hodder Moa Beckett

Published in 2004 by Hodder Moa Beckett Publishers Ltd
[a member of the Hodder Headline Group]
4 Whetu Place, Mairangi Bay
Auckland, New Zealand

National Library of New Zealand Cataloguing-in-Publication Data
Newell, Adam.
A consuming passion : inspired recipes from Le Gavroche to
Zibibbo / Adam Newell ; photographs by Murray Lloyd. 1st ed.
Includes index.
ISBN 1-86958-994-7
1. Cookery. I. Lloyd, Murray. II. Title.
641.5—dc 22

Designed by Verso Visual Communications
Produced by Hodder Moa Beckett Publishers Ltd
Photographs by Murray Lloyd
Printed by Tien Wah Press Ltd, Singapore

Front cover: Saffron Risotto with Hot-smoked Salmon and Red Wine Sauce, page 89
Back cover: Baked Scallops 'En Croûte', page 121

Contents

I dedicate this book to my wife Nicola. Without her there is no me. Cooking is all about giving; my greatest joy is cooking for her.

ABOUT THE CHEF

by Michel Roux Jnr, Le Gavroche, London

Adam came to work for me at Le Gavroche in March 1991 with all the enthusiasm that a budding young chef should have. After five years of classic hotel training he was now at finishing school. He soon shed the excess weight he had around his girth while cooking for the who's who that frequent this bastion of French fine dining in London. His chirpy smile and boundless energy along with a rather wicked sense of humour served him well — even when he was struggling to keep up with the speed of a busy evening service.

There were days and nights when I would shout and swear at him, like all head chefs do; I even own up to probably causing him recurring nightmares, waking up in the middle of the night in a cold sweat carrying an imaginary frying pan and shouting 'OUI CHEF'. I would know, as I too was once a young chef. Although the hours are long and the work arduous to say the least, the years go by at a rate of knots. After a stint working in the pastry we sent Adam off to fly the Roux flag in a small exclusive resort in New York State. As a naturally shy person this was probably the hardest job he could take on, as he had to face the customers and also have a conversation, something that most chefs have a problem with!

On his return, as head chef at one of our sister restaurants, management skills were quickly picked up when half the kitchen brigade handed in their notice after two weeks! A few more years were spent in London's ever-changing restaurant scene, after which Adam went off to Tokyo for a stint within the more serene environment of Le Cordon Bleu cookery school there, before finally taking root in New Zealand.

This book is a reflection of Adam's past and present, his adaptations of classics and with an eye to the future. His recipes in this book are ones to salivate over, and they prove, to me at least, that the hard time that I gave him was definitely worth it.

Above left: Adam Newell at Zibibbo. *Above right:* Michel Roux Jnr at Le Gavroche.

ACKNOWLEDGEMENTS

Among the many pleasures I have experienced during the writing of this book has been the unconditional generosity of all of my colleagues and friends who work at Zibibbo.

A restaurant is nothing without punters, so I would like to say a special thank you to all our patrons. They have created our reputation, and without them there would be no Zibibbo.

A special thank you goes to a chef who has become my right-hand man, Glen Taylor. At the time of writing this book I was diagnosed with diabetes, a real occupational hazard for chefs and a real life-changer. Glen has been the eyes and ears for me at Zibibbo while I've adjusted over the past 18 months to a different life. His determination and dedication is something you rarely see in the kitchen world. Zibibbo is very lucky to have him; he is not only a great young chef but a good friend.

I would also like to thank the cast of many staff who have worked at Zibibbo over the years; they have made up the most important ingredient in any restaurant, performing twice a day like a theatre troupe putting on two shows. Zibibbo is only as good as its last performance.

Also to the endless list of people who supply our restaurants and their dedication to provide us with the finest produce. With New Zealand being so far removed from the rest of the planet, we rely on the commitment and creative talent of our suppliers.

Thank you to Jane and the team at Hodder Moa Beckett for having the faith in me to put all my experiences into print. And I would also like to thank Murray Lloyd for the stunning photography and for keeping all of us calm and focused.

Lastly I would like to thank my grandmother Lily, who with her sense of humour and strong will taught me the basics of cooking, even though I never knew it at the time. My only regret is I wish we had had more time.

INTRODUCTION

My desire to become a professional chef was a natural progression that took me from my grandmother's home-cooked meals to the professional kitchens I've worked in all over the world. I found the same ingredient in all these places — a passion to cook and serve food to the highest standards possible.

This passion was everywhere, from my grandmother's Cornish pasty with buttery flaky pastry, served with Branston pickle, to the three-star Michelin food served at Le Gavroche in London by Michel Roux Jnr and his father Albert Roux. Passion makes the difference between being a good chef and an exceptional one. Yet passion is so often left out of the cooking process. And it is not an ingredient you can buy from a supplier.

If you have passion for what you're cooking and creating, no matter how simple or complicated the dish is, you'll put a smile on the faces of your guests. If there's no passion, people take short-cuts. Too many chefs and home cooks look at certain tasks as a chore and avoid a dish because a certain type of ingredient is difficult to source or to prepare, or because the dish has too many ingredients.

In all walks of life there are many different industries with people working in them without any passion for what they do, they are just doing it to pay the bills. At Zibibbo, not only do we teach people who work for us in the restaurant to have passion for what they do, but we also expect it of the people who supply the restaurant. This includes the plumber, kitchen repairman, the guy who cleans the windows and especially the many people who supply the food and wine.

When I left Plymouth College in England after training to become a chef, all I wanted to do was get out of Plymouth as quickly as I could and move to London. In the early 1980s Devon and Cornwall were a culinary desert. My first London job was at Drakes in South Kensington, an English-style restaurant, seating about 80. The food was well cooked and presented, but it was boring. I still cringe about some of the dishes served at Drakes.

One that gives me nasty flashbacks was a dessert called 'Bliss'. This was a creation from the avant-garde 1970s that was never allowed to be changed, by order of the establishment. It certainly didn't resemble its name in any shape or form — Bliss was a glorified cheesecake made of raspberry mousse with a biscuit-crumb base. I'll never forget the day I first had to make it: 'Don't balls it up Newell, make sure the raspberry purée is warm before you put in the gelatine; don't over-whip the cream or the egg whites.' Well, the gelatine turned to jelly babies and the whole thing didn't set. I knew a bollocking was heading my way and there was not a damn thing I could do about it. This made me realise the cooking game had to be taken seriously and, more importantly, that when making desserts you always have to follow the recipe to the letter.

Eighteen months of 'Bliss' and it was time to move on. I got a job at the Mayfair Intercontinental Hotel which had a brigade of 50–60 chefs. There were huge banqueting facilities, a coffee shop, room service and a fine-dining restaurant … and all this food came out of one kitchen. An important lesson I learnt here was that if you try to do too much, the end product suffers. You can't expect to produce Michelin star food out of a hotel kitchen when one minute you're dressing a succulent lobster ravioli and the next minute you're making club sandwiches for room service. During my time at the

Mayfair I realised that there are two types of chefs: the Hotel Chef and the Restaurant Chef. Hotel chefs are impeccably organised, know their way around an Excel spreadsheet blindfolded, and their main focus is to make the corporations they work for lots of money. They're accountants with chef's jackets. In the three years I was at the Mayfair I never once saw the head chef or his team of sous chefs actually cook. They were only doing their jobs, but I knew that being a hotel chef was not for me — and besides, the tall hats never really suited!

I was not alone in my thinking. In the kitchens of the Mayfair Intercontinental I first met Gordon Ramsay and Steve Terry. We were three commis chefs with serious attitude problems. Our main jobs were making afternoon tea sandwiches and trying to stay out of trouble. After making one sandwich too many, Gordon and Steve moved on to Harvey's in Wandsworth, the restaurant of Marco Pierre White. They would often tell me of the amazing time they were having working with a chef passionate about food.

Prompted by this I applied for a job within the Savoy Group, London and got a job at Claridge's Hotel. I took the job because it was in the restaurant kitchen, totally separate from the rest of the hotel. The head chef's name was Marjan Lesnik, a Yugoslav who had worked at the Connaught Hotel for many years under Michel Bourdain. Marjan was the chef who woke me up to the importance of classical French food. I'm English and proud of it, but most of the food I've been associated with from that day until now has been founded on classical French food, so it was important to understand the basics.

Marjan's executive sous chef, John Williams, could instil fear as soon as he stepped out of the Bond Street Tube

Station a mile away. He ruled with a rod of iron and expected nothing less than 200 percent every day from everyone. He taught me how to lead by example; he would not only explain things, but would go through the whole process with you. John Williams also introduced me to truffles. Claridge's had a freezer totally dedicated to them. During the truffle season in December it would not be unheard of to have over £100,000 worth there for use throughout the year.

After a couple of years I was ready to make my move to Le Gavroche. Gordon Ramsay and Steve Terry were already there and loving it. The interview with Michel Roux Jnr went well. When asked why I wanted to work at Le Gavroche as a commis chef at 24 years old, when plenty of chefs would just go on and become sous chefs at other restaurants, my reply was that I wanted depth of knowledge, not just superficial knowledge, and I knew I'd learn this in a restaurant with classical French cuisine and three Michelin stars. I was offered the job.

There was normally a waiting list of one year to get a job at Le Gavroche, so I felt proud to be there. The first thing that hit me when I walked into the kitchen at Le Gavroche was how impeccable everyone looked and the speed at which the chefs were working. The menu is huge, and some dishes have been on the menu for 25 years.

I started on the meat section and very quickly realised that it was either the Roux way of doing things or the highway courtesy of 'Manuel', an imaginary terminator well known to all staff. When an old orange salt container got in the way on the prep bench, I changed it to a smaller container. At the end of the night I was informed that the container I had removed had been there for 20 years and who was I, this new upstart commis chef, to replace it for something else? During a recent trip to Le Gavroche, I noticed the orange salt pot was still there!

The chefs who wanted to be at Le Gavroche, who were passionate about food and service, survived; the ones who weren't left. It was as simple as that. They were just shown the door. At the level of perfection demanded at Le Gavroche, there's no room for mistakes.

After six weeks I was promoted to chef de partie of the fish section. Michel Jnr ran Le Gavroche kitchen; but every so often his father Albert Roux would make a cameo appearance, only at night or for a special occasion. I realised the power of the man when one night we had to prepare a function for Sarah Ferguson, 'Fergie', in one of the function rooms above Le Gavroche. Albert had to personally serve the food. My part in the meal was to cook the 'Turbot Grille avec Legume Farcies et Sauce Antiboise' — the main event. Albert returned from the function and immediately came to see me in the middle of a busy Friday night service. He gave me a punch on my shoulder and told me it was the best fish dish and garnishes he had served. Every chef in the kitchen that night saw it. The feelings I had were indescribable. Two minutes later he was ripping me apart for not presenting something correctly. Again all the chefs saw the bollocking. It was at this moment that I realised individual pieces of brilliance are not important if you're not consistent.

The biggest challenge I've faced in my career was running the patisserie at Le Gavroche. It was a huge honour when Mark Prescott asked me to do it. The patisserie was like a finishing school for me — until the day I started there I felt incomplete as a chef. It was the final piece to my personal jigsaw. No longer would a chocolate soufflé, a Valhrona bitter chocolate fondant or even a simple Anglais faze me.

After a couple of years I was summoned to Albert's office one Friday afternoon. Going to his office was never a pleasant experience, so I was expecting the worst. 'Newell, how would you like to work in New York?' he said. You never say no to Albert. 'No problem,' I replied. 'Good,' he said, 'you leave on Monday.' This was Friday afternoon, three weeks before Christmas.

Working at Albert's exclusive lodge The Point in upstate New York was a huge turning point in my career. For the previous few years I had eaten, slept and breathed Le Gavroche. To be given a bit of freedom in a kitchen owned by Albert and Michel Roux in New York was like all my Christmases had come at once. The food was Le Gavroche influenced, but there was room to experiment with what I had been taught back in London. We were using the finest ingredients from suppliers like Dartagnon in New York City, fresh foie gras, and black truffles from Perigeau. The customers were paying $1000 a night, so money was no object.

The general manager of the lodge was Bill McNamee, a chef trained at Le Gavroche. Bill made me understand the need to keep things simple and just let the beauty of the product do the talking. In the summer we used to poach soft shell crabs and serve them off the decks in newspaper. Okay, so the guests were washing it down with Dom Perignon, but it was simple. No frills.

One year of New York and it was time to get back to London to put the things I had learned to the test. The Heights Restaurant on Regents Street is where the *Michelin Guide* first recognised me. I remember clearly the day the inspectors came to lunch anonymously, then made themselves known after the meal and asked to see the chef. I was nervous but I felt an enormous amount of pride talking to them. They wanted to know who our suppliers were and if they could look in the chillers. Strange, I thought, but was told by Gordon after they had gone that it was what they do when they are considering a chef for a Michelin

star. They told me they'd be back many times anonymously to check on the consistency of the food, asked me of my career plans, then left.

I was then approached by Stephen Bull to work at Fulham Road Restaurant. The *Michelin Guide* found out about the shift and the Restaurant Maître d' discovered they would be eating there on my first night. It was the final inspection for the guide. The stress levels were incredible — we prepared the whole menu from scratch. But the kitchen team from The Heights had followed me, so we were up for it. The inspectors came and left. The very next day a letter arrived by courier asking me to list my specialities for entrées, mains and desserts.

In January 1995 I received a phone call to tell me to go and get a copy of the *Michelin Guide*. When I opened it, there to my delight were my specialities — Remoulade of Celeriac with Pancetta and Baby Beetroots, Assiette of Duck with Braised Chicory, and Papilotte of Fruit with Vanilla Bean Icecream. And next to the list was the Michelin star!

Dream realised, Tokyo beckoned. It had been a dream of mine to live and work in Japan, and I was able to get a job at Le Cordon Bleu cooking school in Tokyo. My interest was only in the Japanese culture and the different foods there, not in cooking any more French classical food. A year in Japan was enough to understand the Japanese ingredients and styles of food. It is the most clean and crisp style of cooking I know. I ate so much raw tuna that it was six months before I began to enjoy grilled tuna again.

After Japan I moved to New Zealand for the lifestyle and to be with my wife Nicola. When I arrived I was told by a lot of leading chefs that it's very relaxed here and dishing out bollockings is not the way of doing things. A leopard cannot change its spots; I listened with interest while they preached to me, but didn't take much notice.

When I was offered the job of executive chef at Te Papa I was a bit nervous, having never been an executive chef before. I was after all a restaurant chef, so cooking is much easier and more important to me than food-cost spreadsheets. I was told not to worry, there were so many systems in place my job would be a breeze.

How wrong could they have been? Icon was an overnight success with rave reviews, but this was achieved at a price. The kitchen had a revolving door and the chefs were leaving as quickly as they came. Eventually we managed to weed

out the muppets and had a hard core of chefs who wanted to be there, who realised that there were things to learn and strive for. The 'systems' they had spoken of were nowhere to be seen, but the good reviews still kept coming and so did the customers.

Te Papa was and still is an inspirational place for me. It enabled me to reside here in New Zealand, and Icon was a platform for me to show my skills without being too clever. To have things like paua, whitebait, crayfish, cervena and green-lipped mussels to cook with was overwhelming. I would spend days experimenting, like a kid in a toyshop. Instead of making the classic whitebait fritter, which I love, I served Sautéed Whitebait with Celeriac Purée, Garlic Butter and Red Wine Sauce. Paua was braised and made into a velouté, then returned to the shells, wrapped in puff pastry and baked.

I believe New Zealand hasn't yet developed its own unique style, but this will happen over time. The food here can compete on the world stage and the chefs should be proud of what they are cooking and that they are part of creating a style and heritage. I don't believe the future of New Zealand food will be based on Pacific Rim, which is an excuse for doing something mediocre that is more confusion than fusion. It's a good thing to see this fading out of fashion.

In 2000, the Old Police Station on Taranaki Street was derelict and ready for a fit-out. I looked through it, knew it had potential, and — after a fit-out by one of the best designers and architects in New Zealand, Group CDA of Auckland — seven months later on 22 November 2000, Zibibbo became a reality.

The style of food at Zibibbo is laced with French classical methods but uses Mediterranean ingredients and flavours. There's not a piece of pickled ginger or soy sauce in sight. I believe in keeping regional flavours together. When you walk into Zibibbo you find a sense of well-being and a buzz of energy. It is like a steam engine fuelled by every member of staff. For Nicola and myself, Zibibbo is much more than a business: we don't just feed customers; they become part of the Zibibbo experience. Many people have asked me over the years: How do you keep going working long and anti-social hours? What motivates you? The answer is easy. I take so much pleasure in seeing other people's happiness from the food I cook. I learnt from my grandmother that it takes the same amount of time and effort to make something great as it does to make something mediocre, and I use the same passion in creating the dishes we serve at Zibibbo that she used in making Cornish pasties. The only difference is the ingredients.

About the recipes in this book

The dishes featured here are ones I have cooked many times all over the world. They are old friends that have never let me down. The recipes are made with ingredients that are easy to find. I could fill the book with dishes of foie gras, langoustines, truffles and all the other extravagant ingredients I've used in the past, but extravagant ingredients are the easy ones. They're luxury items and that's their beauty. The real skill is taking an ugly piece of beef cheek and turning it into a knee-trembling beauty. This takes skill and resolve.

Not everyone will feel brave enough to cook all the dishes in this book. Don't be intimidated. Try to perfect the dishes you are confident with, and people will remember you for having served them well.

The recipes are listed at the beginning of each chapter next to the restaurants in which they were born, but many have been altered since their birth. Sometimes only the garnish has been used from the dish, or the sauce or the cut of meat. Only one dish is exactly the same as the original: Escalope of Salmon Viennosie. This was perfect the day I first saw it made at Le Gavroche.

Adam Newell

Tapas have been a passion of mine since I first tried them in a tapas bar 15 years ago. I'm a huge fan of trying lots of little dishes, and there's no better way of sampling a selection of different flavours than with tapas. The whole concept of sharing food and trying different things is at its best when eating tapas.

On a trip to Barcelona I ate in just about every tapas bar on Las Ramblas. During the flight back to New Zealand I had all these wild and wonderful ideas for tapas. The tapas platter we serve at Zibibbo — nine different tapas items on a single board — was born 35,000 feet above the Pacific. The tapas in this section are the ones Zibibbo's customers demand the most, and the ones I love to cook and serve.

Tapas

Porcini Mushroom Suppli with Aïoli — ZIBIBBO, WELLINGTON

Oysters Florentine — ROMEO'S ITALIAN RESTAURANT, BRISBANE

Portobello Mushrooms à la Grecque — ZIBIBBO, WELLINGTON

Goat's Cheese and Onion Confit Puffs — LE GAVROCHE, LONDON

Roma Tomato Tarts with Tapenade — THE HEIGHTS, LONDON

Oven Roasted Beetroots with Gorgonzola and Walnut Dressing — ZIBIBBO, WELLINGTON

Salmon Rillette with Capers and Horseradish Mascarpone — THE POINT, NEW YORK

Slow Roasted Jersey Bennes with Kikorangi Cheese — FULHAM ROAD RESTAURANT, LONDON

Cornish Pasties with Branston Pickle — 2 TORR VIEW, LOWER TREMAR, ST. CLEER, CORNWALL

Roast Chorizo and Calamari with Cabernet Sauvignon Vinegar — ZIBIBBO, WELLINGTON

Chicken Liver and Prosciutto Wrap — THE POINT, NEW YORK

Porcini Mushroom Suppli with Aïoli

This dish is so simple. All you have to do is to overcook the risotto rice — not normal I know, but the results are outstanding! I have chosen a mushroom suppli, but you can use other favourite ingredients to mix with the rice. Stick to simple combinations such as mushrooms and garlic, or tomato and basil.

---

50 g butter

1 red onion, chopped

2 cloves garlic, chopped

500 g arborio rice

50 ml dry white wine

½ cup chopped dried porcini mushrooms, soaked in warm water for half an hour, then drained on paper towels

salt and pepper

1½ litres chicken stock (see Basics)

100 g grated parmesan

½ cup chopped parsley

200 g instant polenta

canola oil for frying

aïoli (see Basics)

chopped parsley to garnish

Heat the stock in a pot, and keep hot until needed.

In a heavy-based frying pan, melt the butter and add the onion and garlic. Cook for two minutes on low heat. Add the rice and cook until it is opaque. Then add the white wine and stir while reducing until the wine is evaporated.

Add the mushrooms, salt and pepper. Add the chicken stock one ladle at a time, waiting until the stock is evaporated before adding the next ladle. Stir frequently with a wooden spoon.

After adding the last of the stock, cook for a further 25 minutes, stirring constantly. The liquid should all have disappeared and the mixture should be quite dry. The texture for this recipe is different from normal risotto, which is normally ready to serve when the mixture is soft and creamy.

Stir in the parmesan and parsley, and cook for a further 2 minutes. Remove from heat. Spread onto a tray and allow to cool at room temperature.

Divide into 18 balls and roll these in polenta in the palm of your hand. Shallow fry in canola oil until golden brown.

Serve hot with a bowl of aïoli garnished with chopped parsley.

Makes 18

Oysters Florentine

I first saw this dish while working with Romeo Rigo, who owns and runs Romeo's Italian Restaurant in Brisbane. Italians are so expressive, for them food is life. But for Romeo to pass on this Florentine recipe was exceptionally generous. He is one of the most open chefs I have ever met, and his philosophy is that the secrets of the kitchen should be shared. At Zibibbo we also cook green-lipped mussels Florentine in the same style.

50 g butter

½ leek, thinly sliced

½ white onion, finely chopped

1 clove garlic, chopped

100 ml Pernod

500 ml cream

½ cup parsley, chopped

1 cup fresh white breadcrumbs

100 g gruyère cheese, grated

½ cup spinach, chopped

1 dozen Pacific oysters
(I prefer to use Kawakawa oysters) in the half-shell, washed

lemon and limes to garnish

Melt the butter in a frying pan and add the leek, onion and garlic. Cook on low heat until soft. Add the Pernod, and reduce on a medium heat until evaporated. Add the cream and chopped parsley, and reduce by half.

Remove from heat. Place in the food processor with the breadcrumbs, gruyère cheese and spinach. Pulse until smooth, then allow to cool.

Spread the mixture with a palette knife over the oysters. Bake at 180° C until golden brown. Serve on the half-shell, garnished with lemon and lime halves, and fresh herbs.

Serves 6

Portobello Mushrooms à la Grecque

Portobello mushrooms are very much in fashion at the moment. They have a good earthy flavour but still need sharp or aromatic tasting ingredients to go with them. In this recipe they're braised in the old Greek style with lots of fresh herbs, two types of vinegars and a good dollop of extra virgin olive oil. The vinegars add a sharp flavour to the dish and round out the olive oil. The mushrooms have plenty of body texture and are not easily offended by the combination of the two vinegars. This method of braising using the same vinegars can be used for any type of vegetable, especially root vegetables and cauliflower.

½ cup good quality extra virgin
   olive oil

12 large Portobello mushrooms,
   cut into quarters

1 red onion, finely chopped

2 cloves garlic, chopped

¼ cup red wine vinegar

¼ cup white wine vinegar

1 cup chopped mixed fresh herbs
   (flat-leaf parsley, basil, tarragon,
   thyme)

salt and pepper

Heat a little of the olive oil in a non-stick frying pan, add the mushrooms and fry until golden brown. If your pan is only a small one, fry them in a couple of batches to ensure you get them all nicely coloured on both sides.

Add the chopped red onion and the chopped garlic, and cook for a further 2 minutes until soft. Add the vinegars and simmer for 5 minutes.

Add the rest of the extra virgin olive oil and the herbs, then remove from the heat. Season with salt and pepper to taste, allow to cool, then taste again to check seasoning. Dishes that taste as if they have enough salt in them when they are warm sometimes need more salt when they are cold.

For the best results leave the mushrooms for at least a couple of hours to allow all the flavours to infuse.

Serves 6

Goat's Cheese and Onion Confit Puffs

I first saw this pastry and savoury filling combination made as canapés at Le Gavroche. When the onions are cooked really slowly all the caramel flavours are extracted, and the resulting sweetness is a perfect match for the salty goat's cheese. As with all pastry dishes, you will get the best results if the pastry is rolled and cut out in advance, then refrigerated to allow it to rest before cooking. These puffs are best served warm.

1 **quantity puff pastry (see Basics), cut into 24 discs, 4 cm in diameter**

1 **egg, beaten**

1 **clove garlic, chopped**

1 **teaspoon butter**

1 **teaspoon thyme leaves**

2 **red onions, sliced**

2 **tablespoons brown sugar**

1 **tablespoon red wine vinegar**

salt and pepper

200 g **firm goat's cheese, crumbled**

parsley to garnish

Lay 12 of the pastry discs on a floured bench and brush with the beaten egg. With the remaining 12 discs, cut a 3 cm disc from the middle of each to leave a ring shape. Discard the inside small circles. Place a ring neatly on each of the 12 discs to create a second layer, like a vol-au-vent. Brush with egg again.

Place on a tray lined with baking paper and bake at 180° C for 8 minutes or until the puffs are risen and golden brown.

To make the onion confit, sauté the garlic, butter and thyme together in a small frying pan for 1 minute. Add the red onion and cook on a medium heat for 4 minutes. Turn the heat down to low and add the brown sugar and vinegar. Season with salt and pepper. Cook for a further 12 minutes.

Place a good teaspoonful of the onion confit mixture on each pastry case. Top with crumbled goat's cheese, and lightly grill until the cheese softens. Garnish with parsley.

Makes 12

Roma Tomato Tarts with Tapenade

When I first created this dish at The Heights in London, my focus was more on the colour aspect of the dish, which is normally a big mistake. I had the Roma tomatoes and the courgettes and needed a black sauce, so along came the tapenade. In the end the dish looked good and also tasted good — like the South of France on pastry. The tarts are best served hot, but they're nice cold too.

---

1 cup Kalamata olives, stones
  removed

2 anchovy fillets

juice of 1 lime

½ cup extra virgin olive oil

2 tablespoons flat-leaf parsley,
  chopped

salt and pepper

1 quantity puff pastry (see Basics),
  cut into 12 discs

1 egg, beaten

6 Roma tomatoes, sliced

4 tablespoons extra virgin olive oil

shaved parmesan to garnish

1 cup basil leaves, shredded

To make the tapenade, blend the olives, anchovies, lime juice, ½ cup extra virgin olive oil and parsley in a food processor until smooth. Season with salt and pepper.

Place the pastry discs on a baking tray lined with baking paper, and brush with the beaten egg. Dot the pastry all over with a fork to stop it rising too much.

Spread some of the tapenade on the pastry, reserving some for the garnish. Overlap the tomatoes on top of the tapenade, season with salt and pepper, and bake at 160°C for 15 minutes, until just cooked.

To serve

Dollop tapenade on top of each tart and drizzle with the additional extra virgin olive oil. Top with shaved parmesan and the shredded basil leaves.

Makes 12

Oven Roasted Beetroots with Gorgonzola and Walnut Dressing

Beetroots have always been a favourite of mine, especially the young, sweet ones. If possible, buy baby beetroots and roast them whole with the skins on. If you're using larger beetroot, cut them into eighths before cooking. As soon as the beetroots are cool enough to handle, cover with the gorgonzola dressing.

---

1 kg small beetroots

2 cloves garlic, whole unpeeled

100 ml olive oil

1 medium-hot red chilli, seeds discarded and thinly sliced

2 lemons

fresh thyme

salt and pepper

Cut large beetroots into eighths, or leave baby beetroots whole. Place in an ovenproof dish with garlic, olive oil, chilli, lemons cut in wedges and thyme. Season with salt and pepper. Cover with tinfoil and bake at 180°C until tender — about 1 hour.

Remove lemons, and drizzle with the gorgonzola dressing while they are still warm.

GORGONZOLA AND WALNUT DRESSING

50 g gorgonzola cheese

½ red onion, finely chopped

100 ml olive oil

1 clove garlic, finely chopped

juice of 1 lemon

½ medium-hot red chilli, seeds discarded and finely chopped

½ cup chopped parsley

¼ cup chopped walnuts

salt and pepper

Blend all ingredients except the parsley, walnuts and seasoning in a food processor until smooth and creamy. Add the parsley and walnuts. Season with salt and pepper.

Serves 6

Salmon Rillette with Capers and Horseradish Mascarpone

Capers and fish are a classic combination. It reminds me of growing up with fish and chips and Tartare Sauce. Rillette is a coarse-textured pâté that can be made with either meat or fish.

---

200 g salmon fillet, roughly chopped

200 g white fish fillet, roughly chopped

juice and zest of 2 lemons

3 tablespoons capers, roughly chopped

3 tablespoons flat-leaf parsley, chopped

3 tablespoons olive oil

salt and pepper

¾ cup mascarpone

3 tablespoons dill, chopped

3 tablespoons horseradish cream

3 tablespoons chives, chopped

lemon wedges and dill to garnish

Mix the following well in an ovenproof dish: salmon, white fish, lemon juice, lemon zest, capers, flat-leaf parsley, olive oil, salt and pepper. Cover with tinfoil and slowly bake at 150° C for 20 minutes or until the fish is just cooked through.

Drain the mix well and allow to cool slightly. Mash with a fork a little to break it up (but it should still be a little chunky). Mix in the mascarpone, dill, horseradish and chives. Season with salt and pepper.

Serve the rillette at room temperature with crusty bread. Garnish with lemon wedges and dill.

Serves 6

Slow Roasted Jersey Bennes with Kikorangi Cheese

The arrival of the Jersey Benne potato variety from Oamaru in the South Island is an important time in the cooking calendar. The key to the success of this dish is to cook the Jersey Bennes slowly — if you cook them too quickly you'll end up with roast spuds like Mum makes. Add the Kikorangi cheese when the Bennes are still warm enough to allow the cheese to melt and the flavours to infuse. This dish is great as part of a tapas selection or as a side dish to roast lamb or beef.

500 g washed Jersey Bennes, or other small new potatoes

1 red onion, quartered

2 lemons, quartered

6 sprigs fresh thyme

4 cloves garlic, thinly sliced

100 ml extra virgin olive oil

salt and pepper

200 g Kikorangi cheese or other creamy blue cheese, crumbed

3–4 sprigs thyme to garnish

Place the Jersey Bennes, red onion, lemons, thyme, garlic, olive oil, salt and pepper in an ovenproof dish and cover with tinfoil. Bake for 45 minutes at 180° C until soft.

Remove the tinfoil and sprinkle over the cheese. Place potatoes in a serving dish and sprinkle with thyme.

Serves 6

Cornish Pasties with Branston Pickle

These are the pasties my grandmother used to make by the dozens every weekend. The addition of turnip gives a rustic earthy flavour. This is a slice of real Cornwall wrapped in flaky pastry. You can eat them with any sauce or chutney, but my preference is Branston pickle.

---

1 quantity puff pastry (see Basics)

100 g beef mince

1 tablespoon butter

1 turnip, finely chopped

1 onion, finely chopped

1 carrot, finely chopped

1 leek, finely chopped

2 tablespoons parsley, chopped

1 egg, beaten with salt and pepper

2 tablespoons Branston pickle, or other chutney

Roll out the pastry on a floured bench and cut out 12 discs, 10 cm in diameter.

Sauté the mince in butter until golden brown. Add the finely chopped vegetables and cook for 45 minutes on low heat until the vegetables are soft. Remove from the heat and add the chopped parsley.

Allow the mince to cool in the fridge, then divide it between the 12 discs, placing some on one half of each disc. Fold each disc over to make a semicircle and seal the edges with a small amount of the beaten egg. Dip your fingers in flour and crimp the pasties along the fold.

Place pasties on a baking tray lined with baking paper and brush with the beaten egg. Bake for 20 minutes at 160° C. Allow to cool slightly, then serve with Branston pickle or your favourite chutney.

Makes 12 pasties

Roast Chorizo and Calamari with Cabernet Sauvignon Vinegar

This unusual combination works well together because of the spiciness of the chorizo and the sweetness of the calamari. Be careful with the vinegar: too much and the balance will be lost.

---

extra virgin olive oil for frying

2 calamari tubes, cut into
  extremely thin rings

4 calamari tubes, cut in half and laid
  open, then scored with a sharp
  knife diagonally

salt and pepper

250 g chorizo sausage, cut at an
  angle into large chunks

1 red onion, chopped

3 tablespoons thyme leaves

1 clove garlic, chopped

3 tablespoons cabernet sauvignon
  vinegar

3 tablespoons extra virgin olive oil

3 tablespoons flat-leaf parsley,
  chopped

Heat some olive oil in a hot frying pan until almost smoky. Season the calamari with salt and pepper and add it all at once to the pan. Toss quickly and cook for 90 seconds (no longer). Drain and place in a mixing bowl.

Cook the chorizo for 4–5 minutes in the same pan until golden brown. Drain and add to the calamari.

Turn heat down to medium. Cook the red onion, thyme and garlic for 2 minutes in the same pan. Remove from heat. Add the vinegar and 3 tablespoons of extra virgin olive oil and mix well. Pour on top of the calamari and chorizo.

Mix well and check for seasoning. Add the parsley and allow the flavours to marinate for 1 hour. Serve at room temperature.

Serves 6

Chicken Liver and Prosciutto Wrap

This is a flash version of the 1970s classic Devils on Horseback. To make these look really smart, skewer with a branch of rosemary instead of a toothpick — the rosemary will add extra flavour too.

6 chicken livers, trimmed and
    soaked in cold milk in the
    fridge for 24 hours

2 teaspoons thyme leaves

3 tablespoons olive oil

1 garlic clove, chopped

1 teaspoon butter

2 red onions, sliced

2 tablespoons brown sugar

1 tablespoon red wine vinegar

12 slices prosciutto

12 large basil leaves

olive oil for frying

3 tablespoons extra virgin olive oil

1 teaspoon balsamic vinegar

Cut each chicken liver in half and dry well. Mix the livers, half the thyme and 3 tablespoons of olive oil and allow to marinate for 1 hour.

To make the onion confit, sauté the garlic, butter and the rest of the thyme together in a small frying pan for 1 minute. Add the red onion and cook on a medium heat for 4 minutes. Turn the heat down to low and add the brown sugar and vinegar. Cook for a further 12 minutes.

In a *hot* frying pan, sear the livers in olive oil for 30 seconds each side (no longer).

Lay the prosciutto on a flat surface and place a basil leaf on each slice. Top each piece of prosciutto with a chicken liver half, and roll around the liver. Skewer with a toothpick, or a small rosemary branch with the leaves removed from the bottom.

In a hot non-stick frying pan, sear the skewered wraps on each side in olive oil until crisp (about 45 seconds). Remove the toothpicks, but leave in the rosemary if using rosemary branches.

Mix the extra virgin olive oil and balsamic vinegar.

To serve

Heat the onion confit. Place the wraps on top of the onion, and drizzle with the extra virgin olive oil and balsamic vinegar mixed together.

Makes 12

ARTI'S 1/3   ARTI'S 1/3   Button Onion

Porcini mustard 2b   Confit Garlic 2/3   Onion Confit 1/3

Porcini mustard 2b   Conf Garlic

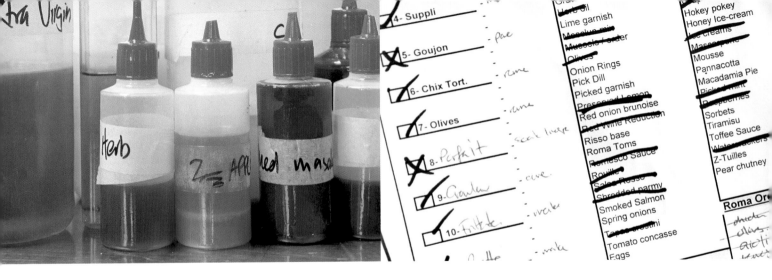

'MISE EN PLACE'

'*Mise en place*' is the term used in professional kitchens for all the preparation work done before service.

I was once told by Mark Prescott, the sous chef at Le Gavroche, that cooking was 80 percent *mise en place* and 20 percent creativity. Mark was right. No *mise en place* and you have nothing; it's all down to the hard prep work beforehand.

Mise en place is about being organised. I can tell which new chefs at Zibibbo are going to make it by watching them during *mise en place* times. They're the chefs who work towards a deadline of being ready half an hour before service, the ones who put the stock on first before starting the easiest tasks because it takes the longest. At Zibibbo, I still drum into the chefs every day how important the prep is. If you're totally organised beforehand, then no matter how busy it gets you'll be ready.

LEPANTO OLIVES

Mary Etheridge

Born in the lap of the gods in the northern Greek plains surrounding Mt Olympus, Mary Etheridge has brought a divine love affair to New Zealand. That's what she calls it anyway. With her passion for olives, Lepanto was an unavoidable extension of her Grecian heritage, something the Olive Lady zealously regards as the essence of her product.

Cherishing the rolling hills of the Peloponnese where she grew up, Mary returns to the fold every year to see her mother and brother — but more importantly to see her suppliers in person. The bond forged with her olive growers is part of what makes eating Lepanto olives like rolling a Kalamata over your lips in the street market in Thessaloniki.

Lepanto olive oil comes exclusively from Crete, where the best Koroneki olives are plucked from rugged mountainous countryside that bolsters the unique flavour of the oil. Sitting in the shade of a gnarled old tree and talking business with the growers on the island is only part of the deep-rooted friendship out of which the best olives find their way into New Zealand's restaurants. This is what the Olive Lady loves — to talk about life, love and laughter with an old friend who sends you home with a bucket of fresh succulent olives.

This part of the menu has always been exciting for me. I think of the starter and the dessert as the real artistic courses. The starter gives the opportunity to really wow your guests with an exciting piece of seafood or salad using ingredients that are in season. Apart from the bread or canapés, this is the first thing your guests will see. If you mess up the starter you will have to work really hard to impress them with the following courses. So my advice is to keep it simple.

Soups and Starters

Skillet Roast Green-lipped Mussels with Lemon and Rosemary Butter — Zibibbo, Wellington

Red Onion and Pancetta Tart — The Point, New York

Crayfish Bisque with Hazelnut Oil — The Heights, London

Roma Tomato Salad with Fresh Crab — Le Gavroche, London

Roma Tomato Soup with Crème Fraîche and Rocket Pesto — Fulham Road Restaurant, London

Scallop and Leek Tart with Saffron and Caper Vinaigrette — The Point, New York

Remoulade of Celeriac with Crispy Pancetta and Roast Beetroots — Fulham Road Restaurant, London

Spiced Rubbed Pork with Tzatziki and Romesco Sauce — Zibibbo, Wellington

Cream of Paua Soup 'En Croûte' — Icon Restaurant, Wellington

Bluenose Ceviche with Dill and Lime — Zibibbo, Wellington

Jerusalem Artichoke Velouté with Crispy Pulled Duck — The Point, New York

Skillet Roast Green-lipped Mussels with Lemon and Rosemary Butter

One of New Zealand's most abundant and delicious shellfish is the green-lipped mussel. At Zibibbo we source ours directly from a supplier in the Marlborough Sounds. The mussels in this recipe can be cooked on an iron skillet placed directly on a gas flame or on a BBQ flat-plate.

---

1 kg fresh green-lipped mussels, cleaned

salt and pepper

lemon and rosemary butter (see Basics), melted

½ bunch spring onions, sliced

1 diced tomato

3 lemons, to garnish

Pre-heat the skillet. Place the mussels on the skillet and cook until all the shells have opened. Discard any mussels that do not open.

Leaving the mussels in their shells, season with salt and pepper, and pour over the melted lemon and rosemary butter. Sprinkle with spring onions and diced tomato.

To serve

Garnish the skillet with lemon halves and serve immediately from the sizzling skillet, which can be brought directly to the table.

Serves 6

Red Onion and Pancetta Tart

My grandmother used to make Quiche Lorraine every week, which she called 'Top and Bottom Pie'. This is a version of Top and Bottom Pie, which I've revved up with pancetta and red onion.

---

butter or non-stick spray to grease tart rings

½ quantity puff pastry (see Basics)

2 red onions, chopped

2 cloves garlic, chopped

1 Granny Smith apple, finely diced

50 ml olive oil

100 g pancetta, chopped

1 cup flat-leaf parsley

pinch dried oregano

100 g brie, chopped

100 ml milk

500 ml cream

6 eggs

salt and pepper

basil pesto to garnish (see Basics)

parmesan cheese and rocket leaves to garnish

Thinly roll out the puff pastry. Cut into discs big enough to line 6 greased rings, 12.5 cm in diameter, making sure you overlap over the sides of the rings.

Sweat the onion, garlic and apple in olive oil. Add the pancetta and cook until golden. Remove from the heat and add the flat-leaf parsley and oregano. Allow to cool.

When the mix is cold, place an even amount into each of the 6 rings and top with the chopped brie.

Mix together the milk, cream, eggs, salt and pepper. Top up the rings with the egg mixture. Bake at 150º C for 20 minutes.

To serve

Remove the tarts from the tins when they are slightly cooled. Spoon a little basil pesto in the centre of each plate and top with a tart. Garnish with shaved parmesan and rocket leaves.

Makes 6 tarts

Crayfish Bisque with Hazelnut Oil

Bisque is one of those luxury dishes you usually only get in restaurants. Don't be put off by the long list of ingredients — when you read the recipe you'll see how easy it is to make. This dish can be served two ways: the straight-up version in a bowl and the cappuccino version, using a hand blender (Bamix hand blenders were the ultimate chefs' toy in the 1990s).

---

2 kg crayfish heads and legs

1 white onion, chopped

1 carrot, peeled and chopped

2 celery stalks, chopped

50 ml olive oil

2 sprigs thyme

2 bay leaves

4 large overripe tomatoes,
  chopped

1 tablespoon tomato paste

pinch cayenne pepper

100 ml dry white wine

50 ml brandy

1 litre fish stock (see Basics)

½ litre beef stock (see Basics)

salt and pepper

100 ml cream

1 shot Armagnac (or brandy)

1 crayfish tail

50 ml hazelnut oil

Crush the crayfish heads and legs with a clean hammer or a rolling pin until broken into small pieces.

Fry the onion, carrot and celery in olive oil in a big saucepan. When they have a little colour, add the crayfish heads and legs. This will be removed later when the bisque is sieved. Cook for 5 minutes on medium heat.

Add the herbs and tomatoes and cook for a further 2 minutes.

Add the tomato paste and cayenne pepper and cook for 5 minutes.

Add the wine and brandy and cook for a further 5 minutes.

Add the fish stock and beef stock and bring to the boil. Season with salt and pepper. Simmer for 45 minutes, stirring from time to time and skimming the top for impurities.

Strain through a fine sieve and return to a clean saucepan. Bring back to the boil and reduce by one-third. Add the cream and bring back to the boil. Add the Armagnac.

Meanwhile, boil the crayfish tail in salted water until cooked. A medium-sized tail will take 4–5 minutes. Remove the crayfish meat from the shell, and cut into 6 pieces.

To serve

Place the crayfish tail into 6 bowls, top with bisque and drizzle with hazelnut oil. To make crayfish cappuccino, pour the bisque into a jug and froth with a hand blender. Serve in cappuccino cups instead of bowls.

Serves 6

Roma Tomato Salad with Fresh Crab

This is a good dish for summer when Roma tomatoes are ripe, and cold entrées are a great start to a meal. Not a lot can go wrong in this dish — it's really just a construction job.

---

500 g Roma tomatoes, blanched

2 teaspoons shallots, finely chopped

1 clove garlic, finely chopped

20 basil leaves, finely chopped

50 ml extra virgin olive oil

Maldon salt

cracked pepper

1 tablespoon mayonnaise (see Basics)

½ bunch chives, chopped

juice of 1 lemon

150 g fresh white crab meat

basil leaves, to garnish

a few Kalamata olives, halved

mayonnaise, to garnish

limes, cut in half, to garnish

Cut the tomatoes into quarters and remove the seeds. Mix the tomatoes in a large bowl with the shallots, garlic, basil leaves, extra virgin olive oil, Maldon salt and cracked pepper. Leave for a couple of hours to infuse.

Line 6 ramekins with the tomato quarters, making sure the outside of the tomatoes are pressed against the ramekin. Pour in all the juice from the tomato and shallot mixture and place an empty ramekin, base down, sitting on top of the tomatoes like a lid. This will help to press the tomatoes into shape. Press in the fridge overnight by placing a heavy board on top of the empty ramekins, and a tray underneath to catch the juice that will spill out. Keep this juice to serve with the dish.

Mix the mayonnaise, chives, lemon juice and crab meat in a bowl and season to taste with salt and pepper.

To serve

Remove the tomatoes from the ramekin. They should be pressed in a disc shape. Place the tomatoes in the centre of 6 plates. Top with a few basil leaves. Spoon the crab to the side and drizzle with the juices from the tomato press. Garnish with a few Kalamata olives, some extra mayonnaise and the lime halves.

Serves 6

Roma Tomato Soup with Crème Fraîche and Rocket Pesto

This soup is great when Roma tomatoes are in season. Try to get some overripe tomatoes, which will be deeper in colour. I add rocket pesto to the soup to give it a bit of bite. Basil pesto works well too.

---

1 kg fresh Roma tomatoes

1 white onion, chopped

½ medium-hot red chilli, seeds discarded and chopped

2 cloves garlic, chopped

50 ml extra virgin olive oil

100 ml cider vinegar

100 ml chicken stock (see Basics)

salt and pepper

1 tablespoon brown sugar

1 bunch fresh basil

6 crostini to garnish

100 g crème fraîche

rocket pesto (see Basics)

basil leaves to garnish

Cut the tomatoes in half and squeeze out all the seeds.

Fry the onion, chilli and garlic in extra virgin olive oil until softened. Add the deseeded tomatoes and cook for 10 minutes on low heat.

Add the cider vinegar and reduce until evaporated.

Add the chicken stock and bring to the boil. Check for seasoning and add salt, pepper and brown sugar as required. The seasoning required will depend on the acidity of the tomatoes.

Remove from the heat and add the basil leaves. Purée in a blender and pass through a fine sieve.

To serve

Divide into 6 serving bowls. Top crostini with crème fraîche and float in the middle of the soup bowls. Garnish the crostini with a little rocket pesto, and chopped fresh basil.

Serves 6

Scallop and Leek Tart with Saffron and Caper Vinaigrette

This is a glamorous pizza with flash ingredients, using puff pastry instead of pizza dough. The trick to this tart is to cook it quickly in a pre-heated oven so the scallops don't overcook.

½ quantity puff pastry (see
  Basics), cut into 6 discs, each
  15 cm in diameter
1 large leek, chopped
100 ml olive oil
salt and pepper
24 medium-sized scallops
shaved parmesan, to garnish
mesclun salad leaves, to garnish

Pre-heat oven to 200° C. Crimp the edges of the puff pastry discs with a fork.

Sweat the leek in olive oil. Season with salt and pepper and cook without colouring until soft. Allow to cool and spread over the pastry discs. Place the whole scallops on top of the leeks in a circle.

Cook at 200° C for about 10 minutes until the pastry is crisp.

SAFFRON CAPER VINAIGRETTE

2 tomatoes
1 tablespoon white balsamic
  vinegar
pinch of saffron
1 tablespoon small capers
2 tablespoons olive oil
salt and pepper

Blanch the tomatoes in boiling water. Remove the skin and seeds, and finely dice the remaining flesh.

Bring the vinegar to the boil, remove from heat and add the saffron and capers. Allow to cool, then add the tomato flesh, olive oil, salt and pepper. Allow to infuse for a couple of hours before using.

To serve

Place each tart in the centre of a plate, sprinkle with the mesclun leaves and shaved parmesan. Drizzle with the saffron caper vinaigrette.

Serves 6

Remoulade of Celeriac with Crispy Pancetta and Roasted Beetroots

This dish is easy and reliable. It's a great combination of flavours, with the creaminess of the remoulade, the salty pancetta and sweet beetroots. The remoulade of celeriac is the star of this dish. As a vegetarian option, leave out the pancetta and top with crispy red onion rings instead.

6 slices pancetta

500 g celeriac

2 tablespoons grain mustard

1 bunch of chopped chives

4 tablespoons mayonnaise (see
   Basics)

juice of 1 lemon

rock salt

pepper

more chopped chives to garnish

balsamic vinegar reduction (see
   Basics)

Place the pancetta between 2 oven trays and bake at 180° C until crispy.

Cut the celeriac into fine strips and sprinkle with rock salt. Leave for 20 minutes to allow the celeriac to soften slightly — it will still be crunchy.

Strain all the water off the celeriac and mix with the mustard, chives, mayonnaise, lemon juice, rock salt and pepper. Allow to infuse for 2 hours before serving.

ROASTED BEETROOTS

500 g beetroots, cleaned and
   leaves removed (use baby
   beetroots if available)

2 lemons, cut in half

2 cloves garlic, sliced

100 ml olive oil

2 sprigs thyme

salt and pepper

Place the beetroots in an ovenproof dish with the lemons, garlic, olive oil and thyme. If using baby beetroots, place them whole in the dish; if using larger beetroots, cut them into eighths. Season with salt and pepper. Cover with tinfoil and bake at 180° C until tender — about 1 hour.

To serve

Carefully place the celeriac in the centre of 6 plates and sprinkle with chopped chives. Add a slice of crispy pancetta and the roast beetroot. Drizzle with balsamic vinegar reduction.

Serves 6

Spiced Rubbed Pork with Tzatziki and Romesco Sauce

The contrast of hot and cold is at play in this dish. The cucumber in the tzatziki is cool and complements the spices on the pork. The dish is topped with romesco sauce, a spicy Spanish-style mayonnaise.

SPICY PORK MARINADE

1 teaspoon ground turmeric

1 teaspoon ground paprika

1 teaspoon ground ginger

1 teaspoon ground cumin

60 ml olive oil

20 ml sesame oil

2 tablespoons brown sugar

1 tablespoon Worcestershire sauce

1 teaspoon chilli powder

1 teaspoon tomato paste

1 teaspoon salt

½ teaspoon pepper

Mix all ingredients well, and refrigerate until needed.

SPICED RUBBED PORK

1 pork belly, bones removed

spicy pork marinade

salt and pepper

1½ cups tzatziki (see Basics)

¾ cup romesco sauce (see Basics)

extra virgin olive oil

Rub the whole pork belly with the spicy pork marinade. Remove the skin and roll the pork belly into a Swiss-roll shape. Cover with the pork skin and roll in tinfoil. Bake on an oven tray at 160°C for 2 hours.

Allow the pork to cool, then cut into slices about 1 cm thick. Season with salt and pepper, then grill the slices on a skillet until crispy and golden.

To serve

Divide the tzatziki between 6 plates, top with pork slices, and a good dollop of romesco sauce. To finish, drizzle with the extra virgin olive oil.

Serves 6

Cream of Paua Soup 'En Croûte'

There are many ways of preparing paua. Some people beat it with a mallet, some mince it and others slice and stir-fry it. As a chef, I'm often asked for my advice on how to cook paua. Because it's so tough, I prefer to braise it for a couple of hours, turning it into a marshmallow texture. If you can get paua shells with the holes plugged, you can put the soup in these instead of bowls then cover it with the pastry. Cook them on a tray covered in salt to keep them level.

---

1 carrot, peeled and chopped

1 leek, chopped

2 celery stalks, chopped

1 white onion, chopped

3 cloves garlic, chopped

olive oil for frying

3 large paua (abalone), shelled
  and cleaned

50 ml white wine

juice of 2 lemons

250 ml chicken stock (see Basics)

4 large ripe tomatoes

2 bay leaves

400 ml cream

½ bunch parsley, chopped

2 sprigs thyme

½ cup julienne-cut leeks, boiled

½ cup julienne-cut carrots, boiled

1 bunch chives, chopped

½ quantity puff pastry (see Basics)

Sweat the carrots, leeks, celery, onion and garlic for 5 minutes in olive oil, on low heat. Add the whole paua and cook for 2 minutes.

Add the white wine, lemon juice, chicken stock, tomatoes and bay leaves. Bring to the boil, cover with a lid, and braise the paua, simmering on a low heat, until soft (about 2 hours).

Remove the paua from the liquid, and put in a covered bowl to keep warm. Strain the liquid through a fine sieve to remove the vegetables. Add the cream, parsley and thyme to the liquid and cook for 5 minutes on high heat.

Slice the paua into fine strips and place in the bottom of 6 ovenproof bowls.

Cover with the cream mixture, add julienne vegetables and chopped chives, and allow to cool. Roll the puff pastry to 2 mm thick, then cut into 6 large discs. Cover each bowl with a disc of puff pastry and bake for 20 minutes at 180° C.

Serves 6

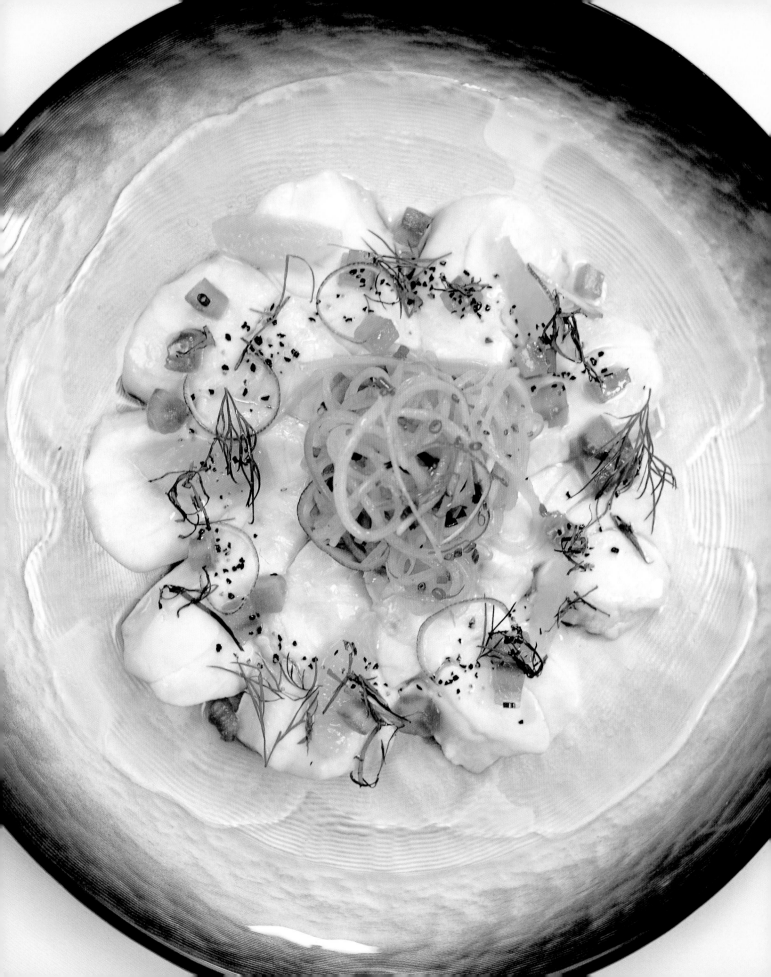

Bluenose Ceviche with Dill and Lime

Bluenose is my favourite fish in New Zealand. It reminds me of the large turbot we have in the UK — firm and very versatile. Bluenose is a big boy and can handle the aggressive marinating of the lime and dill, but be careful not to leave it in the marinade for too long — it's at its best after 18 to 24 hours marinating.

juice and zest of 6 limes

2 tablespoons white balsamic
  vinegar

½ cup dill, chopped

2 medium-hot red chillies, seeds
  discarded and finely chopped

salt and pepper

1 kg fresh bluenose fillets

1 small cucumber, cut into strips

1 teaspoon coriander leaves,
  chopped

1 teaspoon chervil

1 teaspoon flat-leaf parsley

1 teaspoon chives, cut into 2 cm
  lengths

1 cup extra virgin olive oil

2 tablespoons baby capers, rinsed
  well

½ cup diced Roma tomatoes

To make the marinade, mix the lime juice, lime zest, white balsamic vinegar, dill and red chilli in a ceramic or plastic bowl. Season well.

Slice the fish fillets into ½ cm slices and mix with the marinade. Cover and allow to marinate in the fridge for 18–24 hours.

In a large bowl, mix the cucumber, coriander, chervil, flat-leaf parsley, chives and olive oil. Season with salt and pepper.

To serve

Divide the bluenose among 6 small plates, and sprinkle with capers and chopped tomatoes. Place a small mound of the cucumber and mixed herbs in the centre. Drizzle with extra virgin olive oil and some of the marinade.

Serves 6

Jerusalem Artichoke Velouté with Crispy Pulled Duck

Jerusalem artichokes are totally different from the globe variety. But like globe artichokes, the flavour is versatile and can be used in many different styles. This recipe can also be made with chicken. Substitute the duck legs with 2 medium chicken breasts.

1 kg Jerusalem artichokes, washed and chopped

1 white onion, chopped

2 cloves garlic, chopped

1½ litres chicken stock (see Basics)

salt and pepper

2 duck legs

50 ml olive oil

250 ml cream

crème fraîche and chopped chives to garnish

1 teaspoon white truffle oil

Sweat the artichoke, onion and garlic in a little olive oil on low heat. Add the chicken stock and cook until the artichoke is tender. Place in a blender and purée, then pass through a fine sieve. Season to taste.

Roast the duck legs at 180° C until just cooked (about 1 hour). Allow to cool, then pull into little pieces, discarding the bones and skin. Fry in the olive oil until crispy.

Add the cream to the artichoke purée and bring to the boil.

To serve

Pour into heated soup plates, spoon in a dollop of crème fraîche and sprinkle with the duck and chopped chives. To finish, drizzle with the truffle oil.

Serves 6

THE CORNISH PASTY

There is an old saying in Cornwall that there are only two people in the world who make the best pasties: your wife and your mother. I grew up in Cornwall, so for me pasties were a way of life from a young age. They are the reason, in a roundabout way, I entered the cooking profession.

The taste of pastry combined with savoury food reminds me of my childhood and the pasty has had a major influence on my use of puff and flaky pastry in the kitchen. I have always had pastry dishes on my menus. From the simple 'Thin Tart of Roma Tomatoes' to 'Quail and Truffle Pithivier', they have always been by my side, never letting me down.

The history of the pasty is that it was food for the miners in the tin mines of Cornwall, and the ingredients were simple. Miners living on the coast would have pasties filled with fish and vegetables; inland miners would have pasties filled with meat and vegetables. If the tin miner's wife was feeling adventurous, one end would be filled with stewed apple or jam and the other end would be savoury.

Today pasties are sold all over Cornwall in speciality pasty shops. On a recent trip to Cornwall I spotted a shop in St. Ives selling satay chicken pasties. East was definitely meeting west here. My grandmother, Lily Sturdy, would have turned in her grave.

MEDITERRANEAN FOOD WAREHOUSE

Gino Cuccurullo

The Mediterranean Food Warehouse is really just a big schoolboy's lunchbox. For brothers Gino and Joe Cuccurullo a childhood of lunchtimes spent hiding in the corner of the playground with provolone cheese and eggplant sandwiches is a price worth paying for a lifetime among some of the tastiest produce in the world.

The beginnings in the early '90s saw a single palette of goods from Europe arrive in their father's Upper Cuba Street fish shop. Later as the flavours of the Mediterranean shores started to infiltrate New Zealand's conservative kitchens, the boys brought container-loads of canned tomatoes, olive oils, preserves and other wonderfully illegibly labelled produce in to transform the initial two shelves into a bustling Newtown emporium.

The Cuccurullos literally have a 'gut feeling' on what is going to taste good, look good and sell well. The foundations of the diverse range of delectable delights that adorn the shelves in their stores throughout New Zealand lie in the bellies of the brothers. 'Joe and I are constantly eating; we can't stop ourselves. We are always going on a diet tomorrow,' laughs Gino.

The essence of Italian living and eating comes through in the way the Mediterranean Food Warehouse treats its customers to free tastings, cooking classes and pizza banquets. 'It's the way we lived as boys. We'd be at church, then all the Italians would go to play soccer. And once the arguing had finished we'd go home for macaroni,' Gino remembers.

By employing the basic premise of Italian life — eating well — the Cuccurullo brothers have taken the pretentiousness out of Mediterranean cuisine. And on Sunday they'll be arguing over the corner kick before midday macaroni. Same as always.

There are few things in the kitchen world more difficult to perfect than a plate of pasta.

Pasta falls into two categories, dried and fresh. Fresh pasta is much more delicate and takes a little more effort, but it's worth it. For both dried and fresh pasta dishes the most crucial element is the proportion of sauce or garnish, as this can have a huge effect on the consistency of the dish. It is better to have less sauce than pasta and to loosen up the whole dish with a splash of the cooking liquid.

In the Basics section of this book are recipes for making your own fresh pasta and potato gnocchi. If you have a pasta machine and the time to make your own, fresh pasta tastes much better. But if not, you can use fresh bought pasta or gnocchi.

Pasta, Risotto and Gnocchi

Tiger Prawn and Coriander Ravioli with Creamed Savoy Cabbage — THE POINT, NEW YORK

Duck Liver and Truffle Oil Ravioli with Root Vegetables — ZIBIBBO, WELLINGTON

Calamari Meatballs with Tomato Sauce and Spaghetti — ZIBIBBO, WELLINGTON

Pumpkin and Sage Tortellini — ZIBIBBO, WELLINGTON

Ricotta and Pine Nut Crescents with Salsa Verde — ZIBIBBO, WELLINGTON

Chilli and Chive Steamed Clams with Linguine and Herbs — THE POINT, NEW YORK

Smoked Haddock and Creamed Leek Cannelloni — THE HEIGHTS, LONDON

Salmon and Aubergine Lasagne with Caper and Tomato Sauce — FULHAM ROAD RESTAURANT, LONDON

Saffron Risotto with Hot-smoked Salmon and Red Wine Sauce — LE GAVROCHE, LONDON

Seafood Gnocchi with Basil Pesto — ROMEO'S ITALIAN RESTAURANT, BRISBANE

Oven Baked Porcini Mushrooms and Herb Gnocchi — ZIBIBBO, WELLINGTON

Seared Scallops with Garlic Butter and Potato Gnocchi — FULHAM ROAD RESTAURANT, LONDON

Tiger Prawn and Coriander Ravioli with Creamed Savoy Cabbage

Tiger prawns have a subtle flavour, so be careful not to overpower them with strong flavours. Coriander works well as a contrast, especially with the Savoy cabbage. I like to make these ravioli big, about 8 cm in diameter.

750 g green tiger prawns, shelled, deveined and chopped

2 egg whites

¼ cup cream

1 cup coriander leaves, chopped

salt and pepper

1 quantity pasta dough (see Basics), rolled to the finest setting on a pasta machine and cut into 12 discs, each 7.5 cm in diameter

1 egg, beaten

1 cup beurre blanc (see Basics)

1 tablespoon salmon roe

Use half the prawns to make a mousse. Place these in a food processor and blend until smooth. Add one egg white at a time and continue to blend until glossy. Add the cream and pulse to combine well.

Place the mousse in a bowl and add the remaining prawns and the coriander. Season with salt and pepper.

Lay half the pasta discs out on a floured bench, and spoon on the mousse.

Brush the edges with the beaten egg, and top with another pasta disc. Seal well, removing any air pockets.

Cook the ravioli in boiling water for 4 minutes. Drain well and keep warm.

CREAMED SAVOY CABBAGE

2 tablespoons butter

1 cup chopped shallots

1 clove garlic, chopped

2 tablespoons thyme leaves

1 Savoy cabbage, thinly sliced

1 cup cream

¼ cup chopped chives

salt and pepper

Heat the butter and sauté the shallots, garlic and thyme in a large saucepan. Add the cabbage and cook on a low heat until soft. Add the cream and reduce until almost dry, being careful not to let it burn. Mix in the chives and season with salt and pepper.

To serve

Place a small amount of the cabbage mix in each of 6 bowls. Top with a ravioli and drizzle with a small amount of beurre blanc, on and around the ravioli. Sprinkle with salmon roe for contrast and flavour.

Serves 6

Duck Liver and Truffle Oil Ravioli with Root Vegetables

Once you have you mastered making ravioli this dish is a breeze. The duck liver and truffle oil make it a rustic comfort food and a great dish for winter. For extra flavour, cook the ravioli in chicken stock rather than boiling water.

500 g duck liver, trimmed and
   soaked in cold milk for 24 hours

salt and pepper

3 tablespoons olive oil

1 red onion, chopped

1 clove garlic, chopped

1 tablespoon thyme leaves

100 ml cream

1 egg yolk

2 teaspoons white truffle oil

1 quantity pasta dough
   (see Basics), cut into 60 discs,
   each 4 cm in diameter

1 whole egg, beaten

½ cup grated parmesan to garnish

Rinse and dry the livers very well. Season with salt and pepper. In a hot frying pan, sear the livers in olive oil for 2 minutes each side — no longer. Remove from the frying pan and set aside to cool.

In the same frying pan, sauté the red onion, garlic and thyme on medium heat for about 4 minutes, or until well cooked and caramelised.

Roughly chop the cooled livers into 1 cm pieces and mix in a bowl with the cream, egg yolk, truffle oil and cooked onion mix. Mix well until everything binds together. Season with salt and pepper.

Lay out 30 pasta discs on a floured bench and brush with beaten egg. Divide the liver mixture among the discs and top with another disc, sealing well and removing air pockets.

After making the vegetable sauce, cook the ravioli in boiling salted water for 3 minutes. Drain well.

VEGETABLE SAUCE

2 carrots

1 turnip

2 parsnips

1 celeriac bulb

1 cup red wine sauce (see Basics)

2 teaspoons thyme leaves

2 tablespoons chopped flat-leaf
   parsley

1 tablespoon butter

Peel and dice the vegetables into small cubes about 5 mm. Cook in a saucepan of boiling water for 4 minutes then drain well.

In a small frying pan heat the red wine sauce until hot. Add the vegetables, thyme, parsley and butter and whisk until the butter is well incorporated.

To serve

Divide the ravioli among 6 serving bowls, drizzle the vegetable sauce on and around the ravioli and sprinkle with parmesan.

Serves 6

Calamari Meatballs with Tomato Sauce and Spaghetti

This is a twist on the classic Italian combination of spaghetti and meatballs; these meatballs are made with calamari, and are coloured black with squid ink. You can get squid ink at delicatessens or fish shops.

---

6 calamari tubes

40 g squid ink

1 egg yolk

1 cup breadcrumbs

4 anchovies

1 teaspoon mild red chilli paste

¼ cup finely chopped red onion

1 clove garlic, finely chopped

salt and pepper

1.5 litres chicken stock (see Basics)

2 sprigs thyme

400 g fresh spaghetti, boiled in
   salted water

To make the calamari mix, blend all the ingredients except the chicken stock, thyme sprigs and spaghetti in a food processor for 4 minutes, or until smooth. Allow to rest for 5 minutes.

Bring the chicken stock to a simmer. Add the thyme and season the stock well.

Roll the calamari mix into 30 even-sized balls and plunge into the stock. Simmer for 4–5 minutes. Drain and set aside.

TOMATO SAUCE

1 cup chopped red onion

½ cup fresh thyme leaves

olive oil

1 cup chopped Roma tomatoes

2 cups quick tomato and basil
   sauce (see Basics)

1 cup fresh basil leaves, torn

salt and pepper

grated parmesan to garnish

Sauté the red onion and thyme in olive oil until the onions are translucent. Add the chopped tomatoes, quick tomato and basil sauce, and the calamari balls.

Simmer for 4 minutes until piping hot. Add the torn basil leaves, salt and pepper. Mix well.

To serve

Divide spaghetti evenly between 6 serving bowls, spoon around the meatballs and sauce. Sprinkle with parmesan cheese.

Serves 6

Pumpkin and Sage Tortellini

I had never cooked with pumpkin until I arrived in New Zealand. Now I love it. In this recipe I've mixed it with the classic combination of sage and pine nuts. The crunchy pine nuts provide an interesting texture that contrasts with the smooth pumpkin.

TORTELLINI

1 cup cooked mashed pumpkin

½ cup pine nuts, toasted and chopped

½ cup sage leaves, chopped

1 clove garlic, chopped

½ cup grated parmesan cheese

½ cup ground almonds

½ cup chopped Roma tomatoes

½ cup chopped flat-leaf parsley

salt and pepper

1 quantity pasta dough (see Basics)

1 egg, beaten

1 tablespoon olive oil

SAUCE

½ small red onion, chopped

1 clove garlic, chopped

½ cup sage leaves

2 tablespoons olive oil

1 cup chopped Roma tomatoes

½ cup quick tomato and basil sauce
  (see Basics)

¼ cup shredded basil leaves

salt and pepper

grated parmesan to garnish

To make the filling, mix together all the ingredients except the pasta, egg and olive oil. Season well.

Roll the pasta dough to the finest setting on a pasta machine and cut into 30 discs, each 4 cm in diameter.

Lay out the pasta discs on a floured bench and brush with the beaten egg. Place one good teaspoon of filling on each disc and fold the pasta over the filling to make a half-moon shape, sealing well. Place a small amount of the beaten egg on one corner of the crescent, fold it back around to meet the other corner and seal well.

Place all the tortellini in a saucepan of boiling salted water and cook for 3–4 minutes. Drain carefully and toss in olive oil to prevent the tortellini sticking together.

Sauté the red onion, garlic and sage leaves in olive oil for 2 minutes. Add the chopped tomatoes, quick tomato and basil sauce, and the shredded basil leaves and season with salt and pepper. Simmer for 1 minute and season well.

To serve

Divide the tortellini among 6 serving bowls, spoon over the sauce and sprinkle with parmesan.

Serves 6

Ricotta and Pine Nut Crescents with Salsa Verde

Toasting the pine nuts will give the crescents a smooth nutty flavour. If you don't want to make your own ricotta cheese you can substitute with good quality bought ricotta.

---

800 g ricotta cheese (see Basics)

100 g Roma tomatoes, chopped

100 g pine nuts, toasted and chopped

1 clove garlic, chopped

thyme leaves removed from 4 sprigs of fresh thyme

½ cup flat-leaf parsley

½ cup grated parmesan

200 g rocket, blanched and roughly chopped

salt and pepper

½ quantity pasta dough (see Basics), rolled to the finest setting on a pasta machine and cut into 30 discs, 10 cm in diameter

1 egg white, whisked

1½ cups salsa verde (see Basics)

shaved parmesan and parsley to garnish

Put the ricotta, tomatoes, pine nuts, garlic, thyme, parsley, parmesan and rocket in a mixing bowl. Season with salt and pepper and mix well.

Place the pasta discs on a floured bench. Spoon a small amount of the ricotta mixture in the centre of each pasta disc. Brush a light coating of the egg white around the edge of each disc and fold edges together to make a half-moon shape. Make sure the edges are well sealed.

Bring to the boil a large saucepan of salted water. Drop in crescents and boil for 3 minutes. Do not overcook. Drain pasta well.

To serve

Divide the crescents into 6 pasta bowls. Drizzle each with salsa verde and finish with shaved parmesan and parsley to garnish.

Serves 6

Chilli and Chive Steamed Clams
with Linguine and Herbs

This dish is a combination of simple flavours. Trust the list of ingredients below; it's easy to add more, but this combination really works to create a simple tasty dish.

3 cloves garlic, sliced

4 medium-hot red chillies,
seeds discarded and sliced

2 tablespoons olive oil

2 kg clams, soaked in fresh water
for 24 hours to remove the sand

½ cup white wine

1 tablespoon butter

1 bunch chives, sliced

1 cup chopped flat-leaf parsley

600 g linguine (one quantity
of pasta dough, see Basics),
cooked

salt and pepper

Sauté the garlic and chillies in olive oil for 2 minutes, in a large frying pan. Add the drained clams and white wine. Cover and cook until the clams have opened. Remove the clams and set aside, keeping warm.

Reduce the remaining cooking liquid by half. Then whisk in the butter, chives and parsley.

Toss the linguine in the sauce and heat until piping hot. Throw the clams back in and toss well to combine. Season with salt and pepper.

Serves 6

Smoked Haddock and Creamed Leek Cannelloni

Smoked fish and leeks is a classic combination. You can replace smoked haddock with any other smoked white fish, and if you don't have time to make fresh pasta, you can buy fresh lasagne sheets instead.

2 tablespoons butter

1 red onion, finely diced

1 clove garlic, chopped

2 leeks, finely sliced

salt and pepper

½ cup white wine

1½ cups cream

½ cup chives, chopped

½ cup flat-leaf parsley, chopped

2 tablespoons thyme leaves

½ cup parmesan cheese

6 fresh pasta sheets, boiled in salt water and cooled on a tray brushed with olive oil

olive oil

500 g smoked haddock, cut into small strips

1 quantity beurre blanc (see Basics)

1 quantity tomato fondue (see Basics)

Heat the butter in a large saucepan and cook the red onion and garlic for 2 minutes. Add the sliced leek, season with salt and pepper and allow to cook on low heat until soft and limp.

Turn the heat up to medium and add the white wine. Cook until almost all the wine has evaporated. Add the cream and continue to cook until almost all the liquid has gone. Turn the heat to low and cook until completely dry (being careful not to burn it). Add the chives, parsley, thyme and parmesan. Allow to cool.

Lay a sheet of plastic wrap on the bench and lightly brush with olive oil. Lay one sheet of pasta dough flat on the wrap. Spoon 4–5 tablespoons of the leek mixture onto the pasta, top with smoked haddock and carefully roll up into a cannelloni shape. Be careful not to let too much of the mixture escape out the sides.

Tightly wrap the plastic wrap around the cannelloni, twisting the ends like a lolly wrapper. Repeat with the remaining pasta sheets. Refrigerate for 1 hour to allow to set.

Steam the cannelloni for 8–10 minutes until heated through.

To serve

Take 6 serving bowls and place one cannelloni in the bottom of each. Spoon some beurre blanc on and around it, and finish with a good dollop of tomato fondue.

Serves 6

Salmon and Aubergine Lasagne with Caper and Tomato Sauce

At Zibibbo we make these lasagne in individual moulds. If you want to simplify this recipe at home, you can build up the lasagne in one large ovenproof dish. If you're making one large dish, use full sheets of pasta rather than discs, and rather than steaming each mould, bake the entire dish in the oven at 180ºC for about 35 minutes.

---

1 quantity pasta dough (see Basics), rolled to the finest setting on a pasta machine and cut into 30 discs, each 10 cm in diameter

5 tablespoons extra virgin olive oil

24 eggplant slices, ½ cm thick

Maldon sea salt

600 g salmon fillet

1 cup basil leaves

salt and pepper

shaved parmesan to garnish

CAPER AND TOMATO SAUCE

½ cup red onion, chopped

½ cup baby capers, washed

1½ cups Roma tomatoes, chopped

½ cup basil leaves, sliced

¼ cup extra virgin olive oil

¼ cup flat-leaf parsley, chopped

2 tablespoons white wine vinegar

¼ cup quick tomato and basil sauce (see Basics)

salt and pepper

Boil the pasta discs in salt water and cool on a tray brushed with olive oil.

Sprinkle the eggplant with Maldon sea salt and allow to sit for 20 minutes.

Rinse the salt off and dry the eggplant well. In a frying pan, heat 3 tablespoons of olive oil on a medium heat and fry the eggplant for 2–3 minutes on each side. Remove and drain well.

Slice the salmon fillet into 24 thin slices and season well with salt and pepper.

Rub 6 moulds (10 cm in diameter) with the 2 tablespoons of olive oil and place one disc of pasta in the bottom of each. Follow with a slice of salmon, one slice of eggplant, some basil leaves, salt and pepper, and another pasta disc. Repeat this process with the remaining ingredients, finishing with a pasta disc. There should be a total of 5 pasta discs to each mould. Cover each mould with a small amount of plastic wrap.

Take a saucepan wide enough to fit all the moulds in it, put 2 cm of water in the bottom and bring it to a simmer. Place the lasagne moulds into the saucepan and cover with a lid. Steam for 8–10 minutes or until piping hot.

To make the Caper and Tomato Sauce, mix all ingredients well, season and allow to infuse for 2 hours.

To serve

Carefully remove each lasagne and place on a small plate. Spoon some tomato and caper sauce over the lasagne. Garnish with shaved parmesan.

Serves 6

Saffron Risotto with Hot-smoked Salmon and Red Wine Sauce

When I first saw this dish at Le Gavroche, I was confused about how the flavours would fit together, but the saffron and red wine sauce really does work well. I've added hot-smoked salmon in this version to create a really earthy dish, and to add zing I've also added preserved lemon rind.

1125 ml fish stock (see Basics)

1 red onion, chopped

1 clove garlic, chopped

2 tablespoons butter

1½ cups arborio rice

1 pinch saffron threads

1 cup dry white wine

rind of 2 preserved lemons (see Basics), finely diced

½ cup flat-leaf parsley, chopped

½ bunch chives, chopped

3 tablespoons crème fraîche

salt and pepper

500 g hot-smoked salmon, skin removed

¾ cup red wine sauce (see Basics)

salsa rosso (see page 147) to garnish

basil leaves to garnish

Heat the fish stock in a saucepan.

In another large saucepan, sauté the onion and garlic in butter until translucent. Add the rice and continue to cook on low heat for a few minutes until translucent. Add the saffron and white wine and stir continuously until the wine is all absorbed.

Add the hot stock one ladle at a time, waiting until each has been absorbed before adding the next. Stir continuously with a wooden spoon as the stock is added. This will release the starch from the rice and make the risotto creamy.

When all the stock is added and the rice is cooked (about 12 minutes), remove from the heat and add the preserved lemon rind, herbs and crème fraîche. Mix well and season to taste.

In a small saucepan, heat the red wine sauce until piping hot.

To serve

Divide the risotto between 6 serving bowls, place a piece of the hot-smoked salmon on top and drizzle the red wine sauce around it. Garnish each with a spoonful of salsa rosso and basil leaves.

Serves 6

Seafood Gnocchi with Basil Pesto

This is a dish from Romeo's Italian Restaurant in Brisbane. I've lightened up the dish a bit from the original version, which was delicious but heavy on cream. This version is still a very punchy way of serving seafood and pasta.

SEAFOOD GNOCCHI

2 tablespoons basil pesto (see Basics)

½ cup fresh white breadcrumbs

300 g cooked mashed potato

100 g steamed white fish fillets, flaked

2 egg yolks

2 tablespoons grated parmesan

½ cup parsley, chopped

salt and pepper

100 g garlic butter (see Basics)

Mix all the ingredients by hand. Knead into a smooth ball. Refrigerate for 30 minutes to rest. Divide into four, and roll into long snake-like shapes on a floured bench. Using a sharp knife, cut at an angle across the gnocchi roll.

Place the gnocchi in boiling salted water for a couple of minutes until cooked. Drain in a colander and leave in a single layer on a greased tray before starting to make the sauce.

SAUCE

½ red onion, chopped

1 clove garlic, chopped

½ medium-hot red chilli, seeds discarded and chopped

75 ml extra virgin olive oil

6 pieces small calamari tubes

6 scallops

6 mussels, cleaned and left in the shell

6 clams, cleaned and left in the shell

120 g firm white fish fillets

¼ cup dry white wine

1 tablespoon butter

2 tablespoons basil pesto to garnish

Sauté the onion, garlic and chilli in a large non-stick frying pan for 2 minutes in the olive oil. Add the seafood and continue to cook for 3–4 minutes or until the mussels and clams have opened. Add the white wine and butter and stir to combine. Add the gnocchi and heat through with the seafood and sauce.

To serve

Divide into 6 bowls. Drizzle with basil pesto.

Serves 6

Oven Baked Porcini Mushrooms and Herb Gnocchi

Any mushrooms you like or that are in season can be added to this dish. The great thing about this combination is the smell of the truffle oil, which will fill the room when it hits the hot mushrooms.

75 g dried porcini

1 red onion, chopped

2 cloves garlic, chopped

6 large Portobello mushrooms

18 small white button mushrooms

18 small brown button
  mushrooms

¼ cup olive oil

¼ cup white wine

500 ml cream

12 button onions, blanched and
  peeled

2 tablespoons chopped parsley

2 tablespoons chopped chives

600 g herb gnocchi (see Basics),
  boiled in salt water for a couple
  of minutes until cooked

2 tablespoons grated parmesan

2 teaspoons truffle oil

Soak the porcini in 1½ cups of warm water for 1 hour. Remove the water and drain on paper towels.

Sauté the red onion, garlic and all the mushrooms in the olive oil until golden brown. Add the white wine, and continue to cook on medium heat for 2 minutes. Add the cream and reduce until the mixture coats the back of a spoon.

Add the button onions and herbs and mix thoroughly.

Place the whole mixture in a good ovenproof dish and sprinkle with the herb gnocchi and 1 tablespoon of parmesan. Bake at 200° C for 10 minutes or until golden brown.

To serve

Remove from oven, sprinkle with the remaining parmesan and drizzle with truffle oil.

Serves 6

Seared Scallops with Garlic Butter and Potato Gnocchi

This recipe is really simple and quick to prepare. Fresh scallops are so sweet and juicy that they work best with simple combinations like the garlic and gnocchi in this recipe. Use only really fresh scallops and be careful not to overcook them.

1 cup cherry tomatoes

1 tablespoon olive oil

1 kg fresh scallops, cleaned

salt and pepper

1½ quantity (900 g) herb gnocchi (see Basics)

½ cup garlic butter (see Basics)

2 tablespoons thyme leaves

½ cup chopped flat-leaf parsley

Bring a saucepan of salted water to a rapid boil.

Meanwhile, sauté the cherry tomatoes in olive oil in a hot frying pan for 1 minute. Remove tomatoes and set aside. Place the scallops in the same frying pan, and season with salt and pepper. Cook for no longer than 30 seconds on each side. Put the tomatoes back in the frying pan.

Add the gnocchi to the boiling water and cook for a couple of minutes until they are soft. Drain well.

Add the garlic butter, thyme and parsley to the scallops and tomatoes. Heat through and toss in with the potato gnocchi.

Serves 6

THE PASS

The pass is the centre of the world at Zibibbo. It's the place where the restaurant and kitchen come together. The pass hears more gossip than most and it can keep a secret. The pass is where the orders from the restaurant go into the kitchen. It's also where all the food is checked and directed to the correct table, and most importantly to the right person.

When we designed the restaurant at Zibibbo, we wanted everyone who dined to feel part of the whole theatrical restaurant experience. The kitchen is positioned so customers can watch the chefs prepare the meals. It lets all the customers know we have nothing to hide. The pass is the place where the fury of the kitchen and the relaxing restaurant atmosphere meet.

The difference between the highly charged atmosphere of the kitchen and the calmness of the restaurant is something to behold. Sometimes I stand back and wonder how such well-cooked food can come out of such a stressed environment. For me the full beauty of a dish is not appreciated until it is seen complete on the pass after making its journey through the kitchen. The pass at Zibibbo is our quality controller; nothing second rate gets past it.

STONYRIDGE VINEYARD

Steve White

On shelves well above the reach of your average circus dwarf, and with a price tag to match, you will find the unassuming Stonyridge label. Born from a sailor's Mediterranean daydream, the Waiheke Island vineyard is over 20 years old and about as uber-cool as one gets in a grassy field full of grapes. With the sound of jazz drifting over the cork trees, olive groves and acres of vines, Stonyridge is listed as alternative chic, says Steve White, once-upon-a-sailor.

There is no apology made for the reputation of his wines. Stonyridge grapes, pulled from some of Waiheke's oldest vines, are weighing in alongside premium Bordeaux and Californian reds and gracing the crystal of Parisian sommeliers. Ranking first equal at a blind tasting in Paris, Stonyridge's cult Larose blend looks cheap compared to its $700 Bordeaux and Napa peers pulling silver and bronze. And neither does Steve say he has the best wine in the country. Other Kiwi wines also make the grade — just not *every year*. The consistently superb Larose is sold out before the lesser informed wannabe wine buff can even get a look in.

Waiheke is in jeopardy of losing the gracious bohemian bonhomie of old to chrome-plated barbecues and gleaming Porsche off-roaders. But an old mariner and his bottles of booze are holding onto the flavour of New Zealand and giving the life-rich and jandal-wearing people something they can spend their money on that makes sense. A glass of real wine.

I grew up in Cornwall, so seafood has always played a huge part in my life. It is my favourite type of food to cook, because of its simplicity and all the different colours and textures.

Be careful when you cook fish. Because it is so delicate you need to give attention to cooking times. There's nothing worse than a big groper steak crucified because it's been on the grill for 2 minutes too long. Also be careful not to overpower seafood with strong garnishes or sauces. The fish is the main actor, all the rest are just extras.

Seafood

Escalope of Salmon 'Viennoise' — Le Gavroche, London

Warm Salmon Gravlax with Dill and Potato Pancakes — The Heights, London

Roast Groper with Truffle Mash and Garlic Herb Butter — Zibibbo, Wellington

Baked Fish 'En Papillote' with Fennel and Preserved Lemons — The Heights, London

Smoked Fish and Spring Onion Pies — The Point, New York

Seafood Paella — Zibibbo, Wellington

Oven Baked Seafood Bouillabaisse with Traditional Garnish — The Point, New York

Baked Scallops 'En Croûte' — Fulham Road Restaurant, London

Paua Fitters with Mayonnaise — Riversdale Beach, New Zealand

Barbecued Crayfish with Riversdale Sauce — Riversdale Beach, New Zealand

Escalope of Salmon 'Viennoise'

Born and bred at London's Le Gavroche Restaurant, this dish is seen on menus around the world. The combination of salmon, mustard, mushroom and herb crust is so complete there's no need to change anything.

50 ml fish stock (see Basics)

50 ml white wine

6 pieces of salmon, 150 g each, bones removed

salt and pepper

50 g Dijon mustard

mushroom duxelle (see recipe on following page)

50 g tomato fondue (see Basics)

Viennoise cheese and herb crust (see recipe on following page)

wilted spinach for serving

Viennoise sauce (see recipe on following page)

parmesan to garnish

Pour the fish stock and white wine into an ovenproof dish. Place the salmon pieces evenly apart in the dish. Season with salt and pepper and spread each salmon piece with the mustard, using a palette knife. Spread the mushroom duxelle on top of the mustard, top with tomato fondue and then the cheese and herb crust. Bake at 200° C for 10 minutes. The crust will melt and cook the fish.

MUSHROOM DUXELLE

100 g white button mushrooms

¼ red onion, chopped

½ clove garlic, chopped

knob of butter

20 ml cream

salt and pepper

Clean the mushrooms by rubbing gently with a tea-towel. Chop the mushrooms very finely with a food processor (or by hand if you prefer).

Sauté the onion and garlic in butter for 2 minutes without colouring. Add the mushrooms and cook on a low heat until all the liquid from the mushrooms has evaporated. Add the cream and cook for a couple of minutes until completely bound. Season with salt and pepper.

VIENNOISE CHEESE AND HERB CRUST

50 g soft butter

½ slice white bread, crusts removed

25 g gruyère cheese, grated

15 g cheddar cheese, grated

½ bunch flat-leaf parsley

leaves from 4 sprigs thyme

Place all ingredients in a food processor and blend until smooth. Spread out on a greased tray and refrigerate until set. Cut into required shape to cover each piece of fish individually. These crusts freeze well in an airtight container.

VIENNOISE SAUCE

2 shallots

½ clove chopped garlic

canola oil for frying

50 ml dry white wine

50 ml vermouth

250 ml fish stock (see Basics)

250 ml cream

salt and pepper

Fry the shallots and garlic in the canola oil without colouring. Add the wine and vermouth and reduce until nearly evaporated. Add the fish stock, and reduce by half.

Add the cream and reduce on low heat until thick enough to coat the back of a spoon. Season with salt and pepper. Keep warm.

To serve

Place each piece of salmon on some spinach which has been cooked quickly in a hot wok with olive oil, salt and pepper. Top with the warm Viennoise sauce and sprinkle with grated parmesan.

Serves 6

Warm Salmon Gravlax with Dill and Potato Pancakes

Gravlax goes well with both potato and pancakes, because it's been cured in salt and herbs, so I decided to combine the two for a light fluffy pancake. A variation of this recipe is to thinly slice the cold gravlax, leaving behind the skin, and place it on smaller pancakes with crème fraîche. This makes a great canapé.

juice and zest of 4 lemons

½ cup dill, chopped

¼ cup Maldon salt

½ cup brown sugar

4 cloves, lightly toasted under the grill

1 teaspoon juniper berries, lightly toasted under the grill

½ cup brandy

750 g salmon fillet, skin on, bones removed

½ cup dill, chopped

Mix all but the last two ingredients together to make the curing mix. Put this in a container big enough to fit the salmon (but with not too much room around it). Don't use an aluminium container as this will taint the flavour. Place the salmon, skin side up, into the curing mix. Place a light weight on the salmon to keep it in the mix, then cover and refrigerate for 24 hours.

Remove the salmon from the curing mix and wash well under cold water. Dry the salmon and sprinkle with ½ cup chopped dill, pressing it on well. Refrigerate for a couple of hours for the flavours to infuse.

Cut the salmon fillet into 6 slices, and heat under the grill.

DILL AND POTATO PANCAKES

6 tablespoons crème fraîche

1 tablespoon horseradish cream

1 teaspoon finely diced red onion

chopped chives

½ cup milk

1 tablespoon fresh yeast

1 tablespoon sugar

1 teaspoon salt

2 cups wholemeal flour

1 cup cooked mashed potato

½ cup dill, chopped

2 egg whites, whisked until stiff

vegetable oil for frying

lemon wedges to garnish

Mix the crème fraîche, horseradish cream, red onion and chopped chives together and set aside.

Heat the milk until lukewarm. Transfer to a metal bowl and stir in the yeast, sugar and salt until dissolved. Mix in the flour, mashed potato and chopped dill. Carefully fold in the egg whites.

Heat the oil in a small non-stick frying pan and spoon in dollops of pancake mix to make pancakes about the size of large pikelets. Cook on medium heat until small bubbles form. Turn and cook for a further minute. This should make 18 pancakes.

To serve

Place 3 pancakes on each of 6 serving plates, along with a good spoonful of the crème fraîche mix and a piece of salmon. Garnish with dill and lemon wedges.

Serves 6

GRAVLAX

CURED ON 24/2 - 2.50 PM
WASH ON 25/2 - 2.50 PM.

Roast Groper with Truffle Mash and Garlic Herb Butter

Groper is the sea bass of New Zealand — a big fleshy deep-sea fish, which is solid and tasty enough to be able to roast and serve with strong flavours like garlic and truffle.

6 medium-sized potatoes, to
    produce 3 cups of potato flesh

½ cup cream

2 tablespoons butter

2 egg yolks

salt and pepper

1 cup chopped herbs (chives,
    parsley, thyme)

1 tablespoon truffle oil

6 x 150 g fillets of groper or other
    white fish

olive oil for roasting

1 cup garlic butter (see Basics)

¼ cup rocket pesto (see Basics)

2 tablespoons saffron aïoli
    (see Basics)

Bake the potatoes in their skins. When cool enough to handle, scoop out the flesh, to make 3 cups full. Mash the baked potato flesh with the cream, butter and egg yolks. Season with salt and pepper. Add the herbs and truffle oil and keep warm.

Roast the groper at 180° C in a little olive oil until golden on all sides.

Gently melt the garlic butter.

To serve

Spoon a portion of mashed potato in the centre of each plate. Place a groper fillet on top — the mash should start to collapse under the weight of the fish. Drizzle with hot garlic butter around the side of the plate and dot with rocket pesto. Top with saffron aïoli.

Serves 6

Baked Fish 'En Papillote' with Fennel and Preserved Lemons

Try to buy fish on the bone — this will keep the fish moist while cooking. Cooking fish en papillote (in a paper bag) brings out o the fragrant spices and flavours — in this recipe I've used fennel and lemon. When you snip the bags open to serve, the smell of fennel and lemon will fill the room.

six 30-cm-square pieces of baking
   paper

six 30-cm-square pieces of tinfoil

1 red onion, chopped

2 cloves garlic, chopped

2 fennel bulbs, sliced lengthways

100 ml olive oil

6 x 150 g pieces firm white fish

salt and pepper

3 Roma tomatoes

2 tablespoons rind from preserved
   lemons (see Basics)

3 sprigs of thyme

100 ml fish stock (see Basics)

100 ml dry white wine

Pre-heat oven to 200° C.

Lay a piece of tinfoil on each of the 6 pieces of baking paper. Fold in half to make a crease and then re-open.

Sweat the onion, garlic and sliced fennel bulb in olive oil until soft. Divide the onion and fennel mixture between the 6 pieces of paper. Top with a fish fillet and season with salt and pepper. Slice the tomatoes and place 3 slices on top of each piece of fish. Sprinkle with the preserved lemon rind and top with half a sprig of thyme.

Fold the tinfoil and baking paper together in half and seal the edges most of the way around by folding the edges a small piece at a time over each other. You'll end up with a bag shape crimped like a pasty, with the greaseproof on the outside. Pour in some fish stock and white wine into each paper bag. Seal the rest of the way around and place on a baking tray.

Bake in an oven pre-heated to 200° C for 15–20 minutes. The bags will start to inflate because of the steam being produced inside.

To serve

Have all your side dishes ready at the table, and serve the papillotes last. Snip the bags open at the table and serve in the bag.

Serves 6

Smoked Fish and Spring Onion Pies

I started making this dish when I was in upstate New York during the winter. With six feet of snow outside I needed to provide a tasty and warming lunch. This dish is easy to make and perfect for cold days.

butter or non-stick spray

1 quantity puff pastry (see Basics), cut into 6 discs, each 15 cm in diameter

12 basil leaves

250 g smoked kingfish

12 cooked mussels, chopped

1 cup crumbed feta

2 tablespoons toasted pine nuts

1 tablespoon capers

1 bunch spring onion, sliced and sautéed

4 eggs

100 ml milk

100 ml cream

zest and juice of 1 lemon

Grease 6 flan tins, 15 cm in diameter (or 1 large flan dish) with butter or non-stick spray. Line with the puff pastry, overlapping the edges of the tins.

Place the basil leaves in the bottom and top with the smoked fish and mussels.

Add the feta, pine nuts, capers and sautéed spring onion.

Beat the eggs and mix with the milk, cream and lemon. Pour on top of the pies and bake at 150°C for 25 minutes.

Serves 6

Seafood Paella

Choose the shellfish carefully for this dish, making sure it is fresh and the shells are unopened. The trick here is not to add the seafood too early. If you wait until just before the rice is cooked, all the seafood juices will coat the rice. Serve in a paella dish, or pour into a large serving dish.

½ litre fish stock (see Basics)

½ litre chicken stock (see Basics)

100 ml olive oil

1 white onion, chopped

2 cloves garlic, chopped

2 cups short grain rice

3 bay leaves

pinch saffron

2 cups dry white wine

12 fresh mussels in the shell, cleaned

12 fresh clams in the shell, cleaned

3 fresh calamari tubes, cut into rings

12 large prawns, shelled and
  deveined

2 chicken breasts, diced

4 tomatoes, seeds removed and
  chopped

salt and pepper

2 tablespoons butter

1 cup black olives, stones removed

1 cup flat-leaf parsley

2 hard-boiled eggs

6 lemons

Heat the 2 stocks together and keep warm.

Heat the olive oil in a paella pan (or large non-stick saucepan) on low heat. Sauté the onion and garlic for a few minutes until soft.

Add the rice and cook for 2 minutes until opaque. Add the bay leaves, saffron and wine. Continue to stir until the wine is reduced by half. Add the hot stock one ladle at a time, stirring occasionally. Allow the stock to reduce before adding more.

When the rice is ¾ cooked (about 8–10 minutes) add the mussels and clams. After 2 minutes add the other seafood and the chicken and cook until the chicken and fish are cooked and tender.

Remove from the heat and remove the bay leaves. Add the tomatoes, salt and pepper. Fold in the butter and olives.

To serve

Sprinkle with the parsley and hard-boiled eggs cut into wedges. Squeeze a couple of lemons over the top and garnish with the remaining lemons cut in quarters.

Serves 6

Oven Baked Seafood Bouillabaisse with Traditional Garnish

This is a taste of the Mediterranean in a bowl. Choose fish that has lots of flavour — so that it can look after itself when all the flavours jostle for position. Rouille is a spicy mayonnaise made with chilli and pepper, which is traditionally served with bouillabaisse.

---

100 g white fish (on the bone)

12 whole live mussels, cleaned

12 whole live clams, cleaned

100 g fresh calamari, sliced into rings

6 large prawns, de-shelled and cleaned

1 punnet cherry tomatoes

2 fennel bulbs, quartered

¼ cup flat-leaf parsley, chopped

bouillabaise sauce (see recipe below)

50 ml extra virgin olive oil

3 lemons, halved

6 large crostini (see Basics)

1 quantity rouille (see Basics)

50 g gruyère cheese, grated

BOUILLABAISSE SAUCE

1 carrot and 1 leek, chopped

2 sticks celery, chopped

good pinch saffron threads

2 tablespoons olive oil

2 kg whole fish, gutted and scaled

2 tablespoons tomato paste

½ cup brandy

2 litres fish stock (see Basics)

2 cups chopped Roma tomatoes

2 sprigs thyme

gruyère cheese for garnish

Boil fennel in salted water until soft. Place all the fish in the bottom of a large ovenproof dish. Sprinkle with the cherry tomatoes, cooked fennel and parsley. Pour over the bouillabaisse sauce, and bake at 180°C for 30 minutes.

Remove from the oven, drizzle with extra virgin olive oil and add the halved lemons to the ovenproof dish.

For the bouillabaisse, sauté the carrot, leek, celery and saffron in olive oil in a large saucepan. Add the whole fish (heads removed) and tomato paste and cook for a further 4 minutes.

Add the brandy and reduce by half. Add the fish stock, Roma tomatoes and thyme. Simmer for one hour. Blend the stock in a blender and strain through a fine sieve, returning to a clean saucepan. Reduce the stock by one-third and check the seasoning.

To serve

Serve in the ovenproof dish with crostini, rouille and grated gruyère cheese on the side.

Serves 6

Baked Scallops 'En Croûte'

This dish is easy to prepare and serve but it looks really impressive. The pastry acts as a lid, sealing in all the flavours during baking. The scallops are baked in their shells, which you should be able to get from your local fishmonger. If possible get whole live scallops and use their shells. Otherwise buy the shells separately.

1 red onion, thinly sliced

1 clove garlic, chopped

1 tablespoon butter

juice and zest of 2 lemons

1 cup dry white wine

100 ml cream

½ cup chopped chives

20 coriander leaves, chopped

36 fresh scallops

18 cherry tomatoes

18 scallop shells

1 cup thinly sliced spring onion

1 quantity puff pastry (see Basics), cut into 18 discs the size of the scallop shells

1 egg, beaten with salt

lemon wedges and rocket leaves to garnish

Pre-heat oven to 180° C.

Sweat the red onion and garlic in butter until soft. Add the lemon zest and juice and white wine. Reduce by half.

Add the cream and bring to the boil. Simmer until it coats the back of a spoon. Add the chopped chives and coriander leaves, and allow to cool.

Place two scallops and one cherry tomato in each shell, and pour in the sauce. Sprinkle with spring onion. Cover each shell with a puff pastry disc and brush with the beaten egg. Bake in a pre-heated oven at 180° C for 20 minutes.

To serve

Place 3 scallop shells on each serving plate. Garnish with lemon wedges and rocket leaves.

Serves 6

Paua Fritters with Mayonnaise

Almost everyone snorkels for paua at Riversdale Beach and they each have their own version of the classic paua fritter. This recipe is borrowed from Mike George, local resident — and my father-in-law.

3 whole paua (abalone)

1 white onion, chopped

1 clove garlic, chopped

1 tablespoon butter

2 eggs

½ cup chopped parsley

juice and zest of 2 lemons

salt and pepper

50 ml cream

vegetable oil for frying

3 lemons for garnish

mayonnaise (see Basics)

lemon juice

Plunge the paua (in the shell) into boiling water for 1 minute. This will kill them humanely and also help to tenderise them. Remove from the water. Take the paua from the shell and remove the stomach sack and beak. Pulse in a food processor until finely chopped. Remove and place in a large bowl.

Sweat the onion and garlic in butter until soft. Add to the paua.

Add the eggs, chopped parsley, juice and zest of 2 lemons, salt, pepper and cream. Mix until well combined. Allow the mixture to rest in the fridge for an hour, then roll into good-sized fritters.

Pre-heat a BBQ flat plate until very hot. Brush with oil and fry the fritters for 2 minutes on both sides. Remove and drain on kitchen paper.

To serve

Keep it simple. Serve with lemon wedges and mayonnaise mixed with lemon juice.

Serves 6

Barbecued Crayfish with Riversdale Sauce

It's an amazing thrill to bait crayfish pots at low tide, leave them for 12 hours, then pull them up to find a couple of takers inside. It's something we do every summer at Riversdale Beach on the east coast of the North Island. When cooking lobster and crayfish, keep it simple. Here I serve it with Riversdale Sauce — a take on the seafood cocktail sauce that was popular in the 1970s.

---

3 medium-sized crayfish

2 tablespoons olive oil

salt and pepper

chopped parsley to garnish

3 lemons, cut in half

If the crayfish are alive, plunge them into boiling water for 1 minute to kill them. Cut crayfish in half lengthways. Remove all the brown bits from the head. Brush with olive oil and sprinkle with salt and pepper.

Place on a pre-heated barbecue, shell side down, for 10 minutes until the flesh is firm. Do not turn over or the juices will run out, and the juices in the crayfish help to cook it.

Sprinkle with chopped parsley.

RIVERSDALE SAUCE

2 cups mayonnaise (see Basics)

2 tablespoons tomato ketchup

dash Worcestershire sauce

dash tabasco sauce

1 tablespoon creamed horseradish

juice of 1 lemon

salt and pepper

Mix all ingredients until well combined.

To serve

Place the crayfish on a serving platter. Garnish with the lemon halves grilled on the barbecue and serve with a side dish of Riversdale Sauce.

Serves 6

Little big plate

Tapas suit the way New Zealan[ders eat,]
says Adam Newell. **David B[urton]**

[T]HE fixed-price, set menu of nine different tapas presented on an elegant wooden board, each [fr]amed within its miniature square [pl]ate, is a concept pioneered by Adam [N]ewell at Zibibbo, and it remains one [of] his signature dishes.

[L]ast week, Newell shared some of [his] tapas recipes at a cooking demon[str]ation at The Home Store.

"I'd spent time in Barcelona and Mi[...], and was blown away by the food [and] the style in both places," he ex[pla]ined. "Tapas, especially, caught my [im]agination. Everywhere we went, you [cou]ld eat these delicious tiny morsels [of] food. I could really relate to tapas. [The]y are simple and tasty — a concept [tha]t really suits the way New Zealan[der]s eat."

[MU]SSELS WITH SAFFRON AND [TO]MATO VINAIGRETTE

[fr]esh greenshell
[...] of white wine
[ch]opped white on[ion]
[spr]igs of thyme
chopped garli[c]

[T]he vinaigrette
[...]m saffron thre[ads]
diced roasted
diced tomato
[...]s white wine
[...] fresh tomato
[...]es a good on[e]
castor sugar
[...]s extra virgin
chopped fres[h]
[...]ams fresh sh

the mussels,
and garlic i[n]
lid and cook
[...], shaking th[e]
a minute.
[...]ve the pot o[f]
[...]le of minute[s]
[...]s. This will
small pan,
[...]te wine vin[egar]
. Add the p[...]
[to]mato sauc[e]
[...]. Allow to [...]
[mi]nutes.
[Rem]ove from th[e]
[an]d the mus[sels]
[pl]ace the m[...]

ther five [...]
Add the [...]
wilted. Ad[d]
cheese, c[...]
and remo[ve]
Pour th[e]
and puree
Refriger[ate]
allow to se[t]
Take the
palette kni[fe]
Florentine
Bake in
or till nicel[y]
will have c[...]
Florentine [...]
Serve imm[ediately]

ROAST B[...] GORGON[ZOLA] WALNUTS

1kg small b[...]
100mls extr[a]

Simply Zibibbo

Des Britten
Eating Out

A DECISION was made that we would take in the movie *Charlotte Gray* — one of those weepies that women love and has them tearing off tissues to mop up emotions. For the life of me, I can't understand how I didn't zizz off, cosseted in the Lay-Z-Boy-like seating that makes Reading Cinemas in Courtenay Place a vital viewing venue.

Another decision, strategically wrong, was to fill up on some food from the United Nations conglomerate of food fronts that populate the ground floor. I have much angst over hot food prepared at who knows what time and then continually topped up. Who is the poor toot that finally gets to the stuff on the bottom, or does the occasional mix around by the stir of a [...] of the old and a [...]

and other body parts were dry and done for. What's the old saying? Beauty is only skin deep. If you're hungry, treat yourself to a Copenhagen Ice Cream, or, if a little more flushed, slip into Stellar and take on board a couple of small side dishes and a glass of vino. It'll make the movie a whole lot better.

Pledging to make better decisions — we have really eaten some indifferent food over the past few weeks — we called in the rule of consensus which would have us not eating each other if things went down the drain.

Zibibbo in Taranaki St was a decision of unquestioned unanimity. Because of the onset of age, I recall little of our first visit there some 18 months ago, but remember its specialty — a large, wooden, designer-made tapas [p]latter for two or more, giving you lit[...] what they do

Because of [...]
menu of int[...]
grabbed so[...]
yeasty, fr[...]
oven pizza [...]
ponged arou[nd]
subtleness of
from the w[...]
doesn't com[e]

My Port[...]
large and o[...]
up from th[e]
oozed juici[...]
delicious f[...]
cooked th[...]
cheese pol[...]
boosters a[...]
sage had n[...]

At the [...]
from the [...]
ly, crisp [...]
mate of a [...]
est yogh[urt]
cumber [...]
tle crate
with gra[...]

INDULGENCE

Michelin man

David Burton

When Adam Newell dreamed of opening his own restaurant, he didn't imagine it would be in little old Wellington, New Zealand.

WHEN my beloved niece departed these shores in 1998 to work in London, I told her she was on no account to fall in love and marry an Englishman, because that would be the last we'd see of her (orders she almost, but thankfully not quite, disobeyed).

But the flip side to this common scenario is that some New Zealand travellers manage to persuade their exotic, gifted spouses to settle on this side of the world and we gain immigrants we would never otherwise have had, such as Englishman Adam Newell, owner-chef of Taranaki St's Zibibbo Restaurant and Bar.

If your career as a tutor at a Midlands catering college is going nowhere, then, obviously, a fresh start in New Zealand has its attractions. But a driven chef such as Newell has no such reason to emigrate, since contemporary London offers the ideal restaurant culture in which to play out high ambitions. For a start, London has sufficient wealthy clientele to sustain extremely expensive restaurants serving haute cuisine.

When Newell worked at Claridges Hotel, £100,000 (about NZ$300,000) was spent on truffles during the season, which were then served fresh and the remainder frozen for use throughout the year, because the customers would expect them. Then there was the £200 bottle of aged balsamic vinegar, reserved for one particular client who might turn up once or twice a year.

Until he met his future wife, Wellingtonian Nicola George, Newell was already well on his way to the top of London's cooking heap, having [...] a Michelin star for a restaurant [...]

ly upon graduating from a provincial catering college, made a bee-line for London. Ramsay had also decided on a complete switch after suffering the disappointments of professional soccer — he made the Glasgow Rangers squad, but was kept on the bench and never given a game.

So how was Gordon back then?

"Ohhh ... exactly the same," smiles Newell, understandably not wishing to betray more about the friend who, despite his fearsome reputation, appears to inspire and repay intense loyalty.

Eventually it emerges that well, yes, actually the sous-chef hated Ramsay's guts and thought him "arrogant as hell". Not that Ramsay would have cared, since, as far he was concerned, hotels, no matter how luxurious, were simply not where it was at for a chef with ambitions.

Ramsay soon left and went to Harvey's, owned and operated by the great chef who was to become his mentor, Marco Pierre White.

Ramsay kept telling Newell to get into a restaurant, and Newell was beginning to see his point. He started to realise that there are two types of chef — the hotel cook and the restaurant cook.

Hotel chefs are incredibly well organised — in addition to the hotel's fine dining restaurant, they must also cope with banqueting, room service and the demands of the hotel coffee shop. Unfortunately, this means that in the midst of preparing a gorgeous sauce for the restaurant they can be told to prepare a club sandwich for room service.

Furthermore, Newell was determined not to remain in the bureaucratic world of store purchase sheets and food and beverage managers, so, though his next job was at Claridges Hotel, it was in its self-contained fine dining restaurant, which had its own staff and kitchen.

In business terms, Michelin stars can be a millstone because the monetary [...]

BY THIS time, Ramsay and Newell's other friend, Steve Terry, had moved to Le Gavroche, and it was largely through his influence that the legendary Albert Roux was persuaded to disregard all the other impressive CVs landing on his desk each day, and give Newell his first big break.

"Nothing prepared me for walking through that door," says Newell of his first day in the kitchen at Le Gavroche. The Roux brothers, he explains, had very particular ways of doing things — and their way was always better!

On Newell's work bench, for example, was a four-litre plastic container of salt that kept getting in his way, so he replaced it with a smaller one. At the end of the day he was hauled into the office. What did he mean by moving that salt container? Did he, Adam Newell, think he knew better than the Roux brothers?

"It was only later I realised that same plastic container had probably been sitting there, in exactly the same place for 20 years!"

He's a star: Adam Newell in Zibibbo's kitchen. Picture: STEPHEN WILSON

changed. In the 4½ years Newell worked there, the only new dishes were a couple of lunch specials.

Eventually, it became a little stifling, and he leapt at an opportunity offered by Albert Roux, to go on a sabbatical, as it were, and cook at The Point, a luxury resort the Roux brothers owned in upstate New York, beside [...]

should we say tyres) of the *Michelin Guide* rolling, and the inspectors began the drawn-out process of assessing the restaurant for a Michelin star: introducing themselves after their first meal and inspecting the kitchens; if satisfied, returning for 11 further meals and only then making their report.

Halfway through this process, [...]

There[...]
Micheli[n]
the init[...]
with the
ham Ro[ad]
the ach[...]
Micheli[n]
cause th[...]
dire if y[...]

Increa[...]
the own[...]
for a se[...]
left and
time as
school i[n]

In Jap[an]
la, who [...]
make s[...]
theme [...]
British [...]

Thou[gh]
turn to
restaura[...]
since th[e]
they mi[ght]
en route

This [...]
time for [...]
ton, he [...]
the Bou[...]
the com[...]
contract
stages of

The jo[...]
was offe[red]
reservati[...]
with the
operatio[n]
out room[...]

The p[...]
overwhe[...]
but it st[...]
own.

With [...]
vision, a[...]
chic, m[...]
Mediter[...]
prices, th[...]

Hispanic attack

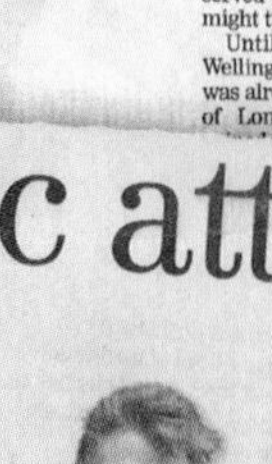

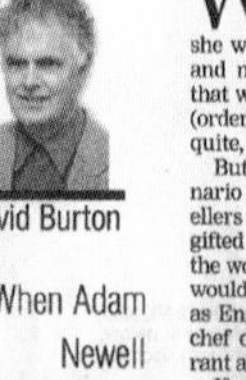

Des Britten

WAS IT going to be one of those nights? I had plotted and planned my dining out destination for last Saturday — a night I rarely like to take in tucker — you know, big crowds, 21st birthdays, engagements, Grandma's 80th and all that. The journey into the city and home to the love nest was going to be responsibly handled by this upright and law-abiding citizen, by means of 'cabbing' it.

Now, at the risk of asking you yet another question that I know you won't be able to answer, why is it that I have to live in a street that no taxi company (I've tried them all except the ones with dodgy names), no driver, whatever nationality, can ever find?

Here we are a happily married little couple living out our life in Island Bay, home-making in our bungalow built some 10 years ago on what was the asphalted courts where nubile Catholic girls played tennis tutored by the lookalike *Sound of Music* nuns of Erskine Girls College.

Well, evidently this once Wimbledon-like neck of the woods, now a street, does not even register as a fly spot on the map and is as hard to find as a pork chop in a synagogue.

Now, 15 minutes late, feverish phone calls to the Master and Commander at home base thankfully had him findin[g] [...]

LOCALE
Zibibbo Restaurant and Bar, 25-29 Taranaki Street. Phone 385 6650

GRAZING TIMES
Lunch, Monday to Friday. Dinner seven days

PICKINGS FROM THE MENU
Cedar Smoked Salmon with Dill and Mascarpone Risotto
Lemon and Rosemary Rubbed Rotisserie Chicken with Salsa Rosso
Bittersweet Chocolate Mousse with Black Cherries

WINE LIST
A careful selection of better buys, also some Spanish, French, Australian and Italian influences. You won't get started under $33. Plenty available by the glass from $7.50.

ADDITIONS
Not greedy. Starters, Tapas for two, $24.50. Others $13.50-$14. Mains, including Pizzas, $19.50-$27, Desserts $12.50

THE WAITING GAME
Very switched on.

AFTERTHOUGHTS
Chef Adam Newell, whose baby this is, has bedded Zibibbo down well. He carries one Michelin Star from his overseas days and on this visit, it was shining brightly.

fresh sexiness of [...]
discovery. Add in [...]
ceviche, mussels a[nd]
olives and caper be[rries]
bathed in different [...]
seemed a bargain for

Pizzas abound fro[m]
the rotisserie had rev[...]
thought of crisp-ski[n]
celeriac mash with [...]
sauce, throwing in a [...]
The rotisserie had re[...]
which, incidentally, [...]
some shallots, along w[ith]
They were gooorgeou[s]
the body.

I must mention a c[...]
Most restaurants coo[k]
requirement that the [...]
jaws to down it. Under [...]
yum-melted pecorino [...]
cooked texture and tast[e]

Could one resist in w[...]
with toffee sauce? No [...]

THE FOOD CRITIC

Food critics are a much-disputed subject between restaurant owners all over the world. My experience has been that restaurateurs and restaurant critics need each other. Critics need restaurateurs for material to write about. And as restaurant owners we need critics to ensure the commercial success of our investment — especially when we've finally got to the goal line and opened the doors for the first time. If a good restaurant critic is on to it, they will know the restaurateur's every move.

It is crucial when opening a restaurant, not just from the restaurant critic's point of view but more importantly from the customers' point of view, that the whole team hit the ground running. Customers pay the same amount of money for their food and wine on the first night as they do after six months. At Zibibbo it was drilled into the staff that from day one when we set our stall out, everything had to be as if we had been open for years. Restaurant critics will soon sniff out the restaurants who wobble at the goal line — and a bad review in the first three months can make or break a restaurant.

In the early days at Zibibbo we had a restaurant critic who did not know what tapas were. These are the type of critics who give the rest a bad name. I regard this lack of food knowledge as hugely disrespectful to the team at Zibibbo who prepared the critic's meal for review. If you are going to write a review that will influence potential customers and affect a restaurant's business, you at least have to know a little bit more than what a Chicken McNugget is.

In the UK there is only a handful of respected writers, and the same goes for New Zealand. We are extremely lucky here in Wellington that the two prominent restaurant critics know about food and understand how a restaurant should be run. Knowledgeable food critics are good for restaurants and good for the public.

3 TERRACES VINEYARD

Mike George

Life can get in the way of getting where you want to go; but sometimes with the right team, your goals can become reality. Classic management-speak — yet, for Mike George, it resulted in one of Wairarapa's freshest vineyards.

In 2000, Mike bought a piece of perfect North Island vine country over the hill from his hometown. With a love of wine and a family long flown the coop, it was just the ticket for a boy who had grown out of the city. When a stroke floored him, the vision of growing old amid his own vines almost died. But the George family wasn't ready to let it go.

3 Terraces Vineyard has become a family business. Mike freely admits that he doesn't do much of the work, but he 'supervises' the clan as they tend the vines, do the books and market the latest vintage. It is a collective nurturing that winds its way through the harvest, production and bottling processes to make 3 Terraces one of the most popular wines in restaurant cellars. And even though all the wines are hand crafted for the boutique market, Mike insists that the wines that come out of his three gravelly terraces on the banks of the Ruamahanga River are made for everybody.

The Wairarapa that almost escaped him has become the richly flavoured life his family convinced him to hang onto. 3 Terraces belongs to the kids, he says. He'll just watch over it for the meantime, and help make a few bottles to pass the time.

Just like seafood, the options with meat and poultry are endless. But unlike fish, each animal comes in different cuts, some for braising, some for grilling or frying, some for roasting, some for stewing, and some for simply eating raw such as in steak tartare.

Whatever cut of meat you use from whatever animal, the most important thing is the sauce. The sauce can make or break a meat dish, and it takes a considerable amount of time just to perfect something simple like plain veal jus. I have the benefit of a team of chefs to help me prepare sauces; but for the home cook who is presssed for time, my advice is to find a good quality stock from your local deli.

Meat and Poultry

Grain-fed Beef Fillet with Button Onion Tartes Tatin — The Heights, London

Scotch Rib Roast with Kalamata Olive Galettes — Le Gavroche, London

Roast Leg of Spring Lamb with Olive Oil Crushed Jersey Bennes — The Point, New York

Chilli Crusted Pork Cutlet with Braised Artichokes — Le Gavroche, London

Braised Pork Cheeks with Sage and Truffle Polenta — The Point, New York

Grilled Loin of Venison with Caramelised Parsnips and Three Mustard Sauce — The Heights, London

Chargrilled Veal Cutlet with Turnip and Potato Gratin — Le Gavroche, London

Lemon and Rosemary Rubbed Roast Chicken with Salsa Rosso — Zibibbo, Wellington

Herb and Mushroom Stuffed Chicken with Truffled Pearl Barley — Le Gavroche, London

Quail Pie with Stuffed Quail Legs and Madeira Sauce — Fulham Road Restaurant, London

Rotisserie Duck with White Truffle and Honey Glaze — Zibibbo, Wellington

Grain-fed Beef Fillet with Button Onion Tartes Tatin

This dish is a bit of fun with a tart tatin (which is usually a dessert). I went through a stage of experimenting by turning everything into a tart tatin — capsicums, chicory, everything. I think the only savoury one that really works well is this button onion tart tatin, which I've teamed here with beef. This recipe is for six small individual tartes tatin, but you can make one large tart tatin by using a large frying pan, then cut into six before serving.

---

3 cups chicken stock (see Basics)

16 button onions, peeled

3 tablespoons thyme leaves

salt and pepper

butter for greasing

1 tablespoon white sugar

½ slice prosciutto, cut into thin strips

1 x 30-cm-square puff pastry sheet
   (see Basics)

1 egg, beaten

6 x 200 g beef fillets

2 tablespoons olive oil

½ cup red wine sauce (see Basics)

GREEN PEPPERCORN CRUST

2 slices fresh white bread, crusts
   removed

1 tablespoon green peppercorns

1 cup fresh mixed herbs (parsley,
   thyme, rosemary, basil)

salt and pepper

50 g salted butter, softened

Simmer the chicken stock, button onions, 1 tablespoon of thyme leaves, salt and pepper for 12 minutes. Drain and set aside the onions.

Grease 6 small ovenproof frying pans with butter. Sprinkle with sugar.

When the onions are cold, cut them in half and place cut side up in the pans. Sprinkle with salt and pepper, the strips of prosciutto and the rest of the thyme leaves. Place the puff pastry on top, pressing down over the onions and around the edges of the pan to make sure it all fits nice and snug. Brush with beaten egg and bake for 15 minutes at 170° C.

Rub each steak with olive oil, salt and pepper, and place on a hot grill until cooked to taste.

Blend all ingredients in a food processor until smooth. Smooth 2 mm thick onto a tray lined with baking paper and allow to set in the fridge for a couple of hours. Cut into pieces the size of the beef fillets. Place on top of the cooked beef fillets and brown under the grill.

To serve

Remove the onion tartes tatin, turning them onion side up. Place on 6 serving plates along with a piece of beef. Drizzle with red wine sauce.

Serves 6

Scotch Rib Roast with Kalamata Olive Galettes

I grew up eating roast beef and potatoes. Here I've shaped the potatoes into galettes and added olives for flavour.

1.2–1.5 kg rib roast, preferably AngusPure

2 tablespoons olive oil

2 tablespoons thyme leaves

salt and pepper

vegetable oil for frying

1 cup red wine sauce (see Basics)

Rub the rib roast with olive oil, thyme, salt and pepper. Seal the rib roast extremely well by searing in a hot frying pan on all sides, in a little vegetable oil. Transfer to an ovenproof dish, cover and bake at 180° C for 1½ hours.

Remove from the oven, cover with tinfoil and allow to rest for 30 minutes.

KALAMATA OLIVE GALETTES

butter or non-stick spray to grease ramekins

6–8 large potatoes, peeled

200 g melted butter

salt and pepper

½ diced red onion

1 cup chopped Kalamata olives

1 tablespoon thyme leaves

Make the galettes in 6 small ovenproof ramekins, greased with butter or sprayed with non-stick spray.

Slice the potatoes into ½ cm thick slices. Trim the slices so they will fit snugly into the ramekins. Brush each slice with the melted butter and season with salt and pepper. Place one disc in the bottom of each ramekin.

Mix the red onion, olives and thyme. Place a spoonful into each ramekin on top of the potato slice. Top with another potato disc and repeat until the potatoes and the olive mix are finished. Bake at 180° C for 40 minutes or until tender.

To serve

Turn the galettes out onto the serving plates, and serve with the sliced beef. Pour some red wine sauce on and over the beef.

Serves 6

Roast Leg of Spring Lamb with Olive Oil Crushed Jersey Bennes

Kiwis pride themselves on their lamb, and so they should. I believe New Zealand's new season spring lamb is some of the world's finest. Remember, the flavour is delicate, so team it with simple partners.

---

1 whole leg of new season lamb

10 garlic cloves, cut in half

1 bunch fresh rosemary

4 tablespoons olive oil

salt and pepper

1 kg Jersey Bennes (or other new
    potatoes)

1 red onion, chopped

2 cloves garlic, chopped

2 tablespoons thyme leaves

1 cup chopped parsley

½ cup pitted Kalamata olives

½ cup extra virgin olive oil

¼ cup chopped Roma tomatoes

lamb sauce (see Basics)

Stud the lamb with the garlic cloves cut in half and the rosemary, by creating slits with a small knife and tucking them under the skin. Brush the lamb with 2 tablespoons of olive oil and rub with lots of salt and pepper.

Bake on a baking tray for 1½ hours at 180°C. When cooked, cover in tinfoil and allow to rest for 30 minutes.

Bring the potatoes to the boil in a large saucepan of salted water and cook until tender. Drain and lightly crush with the back of a fork.

Sauté the red onion, chopped garlic and thyme in 2 tablespoons of olive oil. Add the potatoes, chopped parsley, Kalamata olives, extra virgin olive oil and Roma tomatoes. Season with salt and pepper.

To serve

Carve the lamb and keep warm. Heat the lamb sauce along with any juices from the meat and serve with the crushed Jersey Benne mixture.

Serves 6

Chilli Crusted Pork Cutlet with Braised Artichokes

The artichokes in this dish are braised in the classic Barigoule style. It takes a bit of time to master the art of trimming fresh artichokes, but the finished dish is a great combination — the pungent flavours of the herbs and artichokes contrast well with the richness of the pork.

---

6 pork cutlets

extra virgin olive oil to brush cutlets

leaves from 1 sprig fresh rosemary, chopped

2 medium-hot red chillies, seeds discarded and chopped

6 globe artichokes

1 carrot, peeled and diced

1 white onion, chopped

2 cloves garlic, chopped

extra virgin olive oil for braising

4 coriander seeds, crushed

150 ml dry white wine

4 sprigs thyme

150 ml extra virgin olive oil

½ cup parsley, chopped

salt and pepper

Brush the cutlets in olive oil and rub in the rosemary and chopped chillies. Refrigerate for a couple of hours to allow the flavours to infuse.

Prepare the artichokes by removing all the harsh outside leaves, and with a paring knife trim the remaining pieces of the artichoke bottom. With a spoon remove and discard the choke (the fine hair in the middle).

Braise the carrot, onion and garlic in olive oil until golden brown. Add the artichoke and continue to fry until golden. Add the coriander seeds, white wine, thyme and extra virgin olive oil. Simmer until the artichokes are tender. Add the chopped parsley and season with salt and pepper to taste.

To serve

Chargrill the pork cutlets until medium. Don't overcook, or they'll dry out. Arrange the artichokes on 6 serving plates and top with a cutlet. You don't need to use any sauce with this. The juices from the artichoke will moisten it sufficiently.

Serves 6

Braised Pork Cheeks with Sage and Truffle Polenta

This recipe uses two of my favourite ingredients, polenta and slowly braised meat, to create a really warming winter dish. Cheeks are the best cut of meat for braising. You can use ox cheeks instead of pork in this recipe and braise them in the same way.

---

12 pork cheeks, trimmed of excess fat and sinew

½ cup salt

4 tablespoons olive oil

1 red onion, chopped

1 carrot, peeled and chopped

1 stick celery, chopped

2 cups red wine

2 tablespoons thyme leaves

3 cups chicken stock (see Basics)

salt and pepper

3 roasted red onions, cut into quarters to garnish

SAGE AND TRUFFLE POLENTA

2 cups chicken stock (see Basics)

1 cup full cream milk

1 cup instant polenta

½ cup grated parmesan

2 tablespoons butter

3 tablespoons chopped sage leaves

2 tablespoons white truffle oil

salt and pepper

Rub the pork cheeks in the ½ cup of salt, place in a bowl and cover with cold water. Soak for 2–3 hours. Drain and dry well.

In a hot frying pan, sear the pork cheeks on all sides in olive oil. Don't over-crowd the pan — this might mean doing several batches. Make sure the pork cheeks are nicely browned to get maximum flavour. Remove and set aside.

In the same pan, sauté the vegetables until golden brown. Add the wine and thyme and reduce by half.

Transfer the vegetables to an ovenproof dish and place the pork on top. Pour chicken stock over it and cover. Bake at 160° C for 3 hours or until the pork is tender. Remove the pork carefully and keep warm.

Strain the cooking liquid through a fine sieve into a small saucepan. Reduce on low heat until you have 1 cup. Skim off any excess fat and season with salt and pepper.

Bring the chicken stock and milk to the boil together. Add the polenta all in one go, using a wooden spoon to mix well and beat out any lumps. Continue to cook for 3–4 minutes until smooth, stirring constantly. Add some grated parmesan, butter, sage and truffle oil and season well with salt and pepper. Serve immediately, garnished with the rest of the parmesan.

To serve

Spoon the polenta onto each of 6 serving plates and top with 2 pork cheeks. Drizzle some of the sauce on and over the pork. Garnish with the red onion quarters.

Serves 6

Grilled Loin of Venison with Caramelised Parsnips and Three Mustard Sauce

In this recipe the venison loin is grilled on the barbecue. Keep it rare to appreciate the delicate flavour. Also, caramelise the parsnips really well — I use a non-stick wok to get them crispy. The mustards cut the richness of the venison and parsnips.

3 parsnips

1 red onion, chopped

2 cloves garlic, chopped

1 tablespoon butter

6 slices pancetta, finely chopped

salt and pepper

½ cup chopped flat-leaf parsley

1 kg venison loin, cut into
   6 pieces

THREE MUSTARD SAUCE

½ white onion, chopped

1 clove garlic, chopped

1 tablespoon butter

1 teaspoon grain mustard

1 teaspoon Dijon mustard

1 teaspoon tarragon mustard

250 ml beef stock (see Basics)

1 Granny Smith apple, diced

1 knob of butter

Peel the parsnips and remove the core. Dice and blanch in boiling water until cooked (about 5 minutes).

In a non-stick frying pan, sauté the red onion and garlic in the butter until golden brown. Add the chopped pancetta and parsnips. Cook until the parsnips are caramelised. Season with salt and pepper, and add the chopped parsley. Keep warm.

Barbecue the venison until medium rare. Allow to rest for a couple of minutes, then slice in half.

Sweat the onion and garlic in the tablespoon of butter until soft. Add the mustards and beef stock and reduce until the mixture coats the back of a spoon. Add the diced apple and knob of butter, and simmer for 2 minutes or until the apple is soft.

To serve

Place the caramelised parsnips in the centre of 6 plates. Top each with the venison pieces, and drizzle with the mustard sauce.

Serves 6

Chargrilled Veal Cutlet with Turnip and Potato Gratin

This dish has two homes — the veal cutlet recipe originated from Le Gavroche, London and the gratin from The Point in New York. The gratin is a classic dauphinoise with the addition of turnips, which give a deliciously earthy flavour.

6 veal cutlets

2 tablespoons thyme leaves

4 tablespoons olive oil

4 potatoes, peeled

2 turnips, peeled

salt and pepper

1 red onion, diced

2 cloves garlic, chopped

½ cup white wine

½ cup cream

½ cup chopped parsley

1 cup grated parmesan cheese

whole roasted garlic cloves to
    garnish

Rub the veal cutlets with thyme and 2 tablespoons of olive oil. Allow to marinate for two hours.

Slice the potatoes and turnips as thinly as possible and season well with salt and pepper. Lay out on an oiled ovenproof dish, overlapping the slices.

Sauté the red onion and garlic in olive oil for 3 minutes. Add the white wine and reduce by half. Add the cream and chopped parsley. Season with salt and pepper, then pour over the potatoes. Sprinkle with parmesan and bake at 180°C for 20–30 minutes until golden brown.

Chargrill or barbecue the veal cutlets until cooked to taste.

VEAL JUS WITH ONIONS

1 cup diced red onion

1 clove garlic, chopped

1 teaspoon olive oil

1 cup white wine

4 cups beef stock (see Basics)

½ cup chicken stock (see Basics)

2 bay leaves

2 sprigs thyme

salt and pepper

In a large saucepan, sweat the onion and garlic in olive oil. Add the white wine, beef stock, chicken stock, bay leaves and thyme. Reduce by half.

Remove the bay leaves and thyme sprigs. Season with salt and pepper.

To serve

Place a good spoonful of gratin on each plate with a veal cutlet, and spoon some onion sauce on and over the veal. Garnish with whole roasted garlic cloves.

Serves 6

Lemon and Rosemary Rubbed Roast Chicken with Salsa Rosso

At Zibibbo, we serve this chicken with Garlic Confit Mashed Potato, but roast potatoes would be great too. This has been on the menu at Zibibbo since we opened and it's one of those dishes our regular customers demand again and again.

2 lemons

1 bunch parsley

2 medium-hot chillies

2 cloves garlic

50 ml olive oil

salt and pepper

50 ml white wine vinegar

2 medium-sized chickens

onion gravy (see Basics)

Blend the whole lemons, parsley, chillies, garlic, olive oil, salt, pepper and vinegar in a food processor until it becomes a paste (it should look like pesto). Rub the chicken skin underneath and outside with the lemon mixture. To rub underneath the skin, run your finger between the skin and the flesh, forcing the marinade under the skin. Allow to marinate for a few hours.

Roast at 180° C until cooked through, continually basting the chicken as it cooks.

SALSA ROSSO

100 ml quick tomato and basil
  sauce (see Basics)

25 ml extra virgin olive oil

½ red onion, finely chopped

½ clove garlic, chopped

10 large basil leaves, cut into
  fine strips

¼ cup chopped coriander

juice of 1 lemon

½ roast red capsicum, peeled
  and diced

salt and pepper

Combine all the ingredients in a bowl and allow to infuse for at least 2 hours. Serve the salsa at room temperature.

To serve

Serve the chicken with onion gravy and top with a dollop of salsa rosso.

Serves 6

Herb and Mushroom Stuffed Chicken with Truffled Pearl Barley

Pearl barley is rather an old-fashioned ingredient, but when it's braised slowly like this it has a wonderful nutty flavour.

six 30-cm sheets of crêpine

1 red onion, chopped

2 cloves garlic, crushed

2 cups finely chopped Portobello
  mushrooms

3 tablespoons olive oil

1 cup chicken mince

2 tablespoons chopped sage

½ cup flat-leaf parsley

½ cup fresh breadcrumbs

2 egg yolks

salt and pepper

6 free-range chicken legs

extra virgin olive oil for searing

TRUFFLED PEARL BARLEY

1 cup diced vegetables (carrot,
  turnip and celery)

1 red onion, diced

1 tablespoon garlic, chopped

3 tablespoons thyme leaves

2 tablespoons olive oil

2 cups pearl barley

1 litre chicken stock (see Basics)

salt and pepper

2 tablespoons butter

1 cup chopped parsley

2 tablespoons truffle oil

Soak the crêpine in cold water for 24 hours before use. (Alternatively, you can secure the chicken with bamboo skewers.)

Sauté the onion, garlic and mushrooms in olive oil in a hot frying pan for 4 minutes. Allow to cool.

In a mixing bowl combine the mushroom mixture, chicken mince, herbs, breadcrumbs and egg yolks. Mix well and season with salt and pepper.

Remove the thigh bones from the chicken with a sharp knife (leave the drumstick bone in). Place the chicken legs skin side down on a chopping board. Season with salt and pepper. Spoon 3 tablespoons of the mince and mushroom mix on each leg. Roll the chicken around the mix to form a sausage. Lay each chicken parcel on a sheet of crêpine, and re-roll like a sausage. Tie the crêpine with string.

Heat a little olive oil in a frying pan over medium heat. Seal the chicken parcels by frying for a couple of minutes on all sides until golden brown. Transfer to an ovenproof dish, cover, and roast for 30 minutes at 180°C. Allow to rest for 10 minutes.

To prepare the Truffled Pearl Barley, sauté the vegetables, onion, garlic and thyme in olive oil for 3–4 minutes in a large saucepan. Add the pearl barley and chicken stock. Season with salt and pepper.

Pour into a large ovenproof dish, cover and bake at 170°C for 45 minutes. Remove from the oven and stir in the butter, parsley and truffle oil.

To serve

Place a good spoon of pearl barley on each serving plate alongside the chicken. Add some of the sauce from the pearl barley.

Serves 6

Quail Pie with Stuffed Quail Legs and Madeira Sauce

At Zibibbo we make several game pies during the year. Quail is my favourite. We use quail from the Rangitikei area of New Zealand, which are plump and full of flavour.

500 g chicken mince

1 red onion, diced

1 clove garlic, chopped

2 tablespoons truffle oil

2 tablespoons thyme leaves

salt and pepper

olive oil for frying

1 quantity puff pastry (see Basics), rolled out to 2 mm and cut into 12 large discs

breasts and legs from 6 quail

1 egg, beaten

1 large sheet crêpine (available by order from butchers), soaked in cold water for ½ an hour

vegetable oil for searing

wilted spinach to serve

Pre-heat oven to 180° C.

Mix the chicken mince, red onion, garlic, truffle oil and thyme. Season well with salt and pepper.

Season the quail breasts with salt and pepper, then seal in a hot frying pan, by frying on each side for a couple of minutes.

Place 6 pastry discs on a greased oven tray. Top each disc with a spoonful of the chicken mixture, 2 quail breasts and then top with more chicken mixture. Reserve some of the chicken mixture for the legs.

Brush the edges of the pastry discs with beaten egg and place a second disc of pastry on top of the filling. Seal the pastry discs together well and trim off any excess. Set the pies aside.

Take the bone out of the quail legs using a sharp knife, and stuff with chicken mixture along where the bone was. Roll the quail meat around the chicken mixture.

Cut the crêpine into 12 squares about 5 cm square. Place each filled leg in the middle of a piece of crêpine and roll up like a sausage. Sauté on all sides for a couple of minutes until golden brown.

Brush the top of each pie with beaten egg. Bake the legs and pies at 180° C until golden brown. The legs take 7–8 minutes and the pies take 12–15 minutes.

MADEIRA SAUCE

1 onion, chopped

1 carrot, chopped

2 sprigs thyme

1 cup Madeira

quail bones, roasted at 180° C for 10 minutes

4 cups beef stock (see Basics)

Sauté the vegetables and thyme in a large saucepan in vegetable oil until golden brown and caramelised. Add the Madeira, and scrape off any bits stuck to the bottom of the saucepan. Reduce by half on a medium heat.

Add the roasted quail bones and beef stock. Simmer for 1 hour. Strain the stock through a fine sieve and return to a clean saucepan. Reduce by two-thirds.

To serve

Place the pie on a little wilted spinach. Slice the quail legs and arrange on the plate. Drizzle with Madeira sauce.

Serves 6

Rotisserie Duck with White Truffle and Honey Glaze

White truffle and honey is a classic Italian combination. The pungent truffle and sweet honey go so well together. Note that the duck takes 12 hours to prepare before cooking. As well as being great with duck, the white truffle and honey combination is also delicious on toasted brioche with vanilla icecream.

1 large whole duck (2.2–2.6 kg)

salt and pepper

25 ml white truffle oil

3 tablespoons liquid honey, warmed

½ cup Kalamata olives, pitted and chopped

1½ cups duck sauce (see Basics)

To prepare the duck, remove the wing tips and feet (use these for the duck sauce). Rub the duck well with salt and pepper, outside and in the cavity.

Bring a saucepan of water to the boil — it must be big enough to hold the duck. Plunge the duck into the boiling water for 4 minutes. Remove and allow the duck to sit in a cool airy place for 12 hours. This will allow the skin to tighten to the meat.

Place the duck on a pre-heated rotisserie at about 170°C and cook for 40–45 minutes, checking the heat frequently to make sure the duck doesn't burn. While the duck is cooking, prick the skin about every 20 minutes to release the fat. When the duck is nearly cooked, begin basting frequently with the truffle oil and honey mixed together. This will give the duck a nice golden glaze.

To serve

Heat the duck sauce and mix in the chopped olives. Slice the duck and serve with the duck sauce. At Zibibbo we serve this dish with seared polenta, which is a soft polenta set in a tray, then cut into squares and seared in a frying pan with olive oil.

Serves 6

2004

GREAT BRITAIN
& IRELAND

NEW!
BIB HOTEL

HOTELS & RESTAURANTS

MICHELIN

HOTELS & RESTAURANTS

GREAT BRITAIN
& IRELAND
2004

MICHELIN
Travel Publications

THE *MICHELIN GUIDE*

I've seen famous chefs frying the *Michelin Guide* in a wok in protest at not receiving the ultimate accolade from it. But for the generation of chefs I grew up with, the *Michelin Guide* was the be-all and end-all — the bible according to a tyre company from France.

The *Michelin Guide* has, without any question of a doubt, raised the level of cooking in the countries where it is represented more than any television cooking series star has. I was fortunate enough to gain One Star Michelin status at Fulham Road in London. The effort it takes to achieve just one star is incredible. To go on to get two and three stars is a true test of resolve and commitment, something very few people can dream of. To knock the guide is a sign of ignorance and weakness.

Some food critics and chefs used to say that the generation of chefs I grew up with only cooked for the guides instead of the customers. Not true. I never once decided to chase fashion around a plate to please a food critic. I was taught by Albert and Michel Roux Jnr that customers always come first.

New Zealand needs a guidebook with clout, dedicated to reviewing restaurants. A guide, in the true sense of the word, would give customers more information than a restaurant review section in a magazine and it would give young chefs a dream to chase. I believe that a New Zealand edition of the *Michelin Guide* would be a good thing for the dining public in this country.

Customers often ask me what it takes to achieve a Michelin star. The key is to achieve perfection day in, day out. There's no point being a superstar one day and a muppet the next; customers want consistency. Chefs who cook professionally should realise it is all about keeping standards as high as possible 365 days of the year.

ANGUSPURE

Guy Sargent

Next time you are in San Francisco looking for a juicy beefcake, you might find yourself wrapping your lips around a piece of prime Aotearoa meat. AngusPure is New Zealand's premium grass-fed beef. And San Francisco takes most of it, to feed a demand for one of the sexiest flavours of steak to be seared and savoured.

Pulled from the non-specific cluster of beef cuts on the supermarket shelf and furnished with an identity more appropriate to its ancient Scottish lineage and sublime superiority, AngusPure beef is from one of the oldest cattle breeds in the world and has a fine ancestry of succulence. General manager Guy Sargent could almost rattle off the DNA sequence for Angus cattle; but he doesn't, talking instead about the 500 breeders in New Zealand who deliver Angus purebreds for the brand and turn out some of the best backsteaks in the world.

New Zealand sees about one-third of the quality AngusPure beef produced. You might not know you are eating it until your tastebuds slide into a trance and you ask the waiter where the finely marbled rib-eye dancing in your mouth came from. AngusPure is bred solely for beef — no old dairy cow is going to sparkle like this.

POHANGINA VALLEY VENISON

Robin Ferguson

Pohangina Valley has been voted one of the most beautiful vistas in New Zealand. In a search for his own piece of paradise Robin Ferguson broke free from the sterile world of contract cleaning at Te Papa to escape to this secluded corner of Manawatu and farm venison.

On the 24-ha property, nestled among native bush, roam herds of purebred English Warnham deer — quite the deer to have apparently. In fact, Her Royal Highness Queen Elizabeth II is fond of this particular breed of Bambi.

Indeed Pohangina Valley Venison looks after its deer as if they were blue-blooded themselves. With a free-range focus, Robin makes a point of not overly handling the deer, preferring to leave them to the rhythm of Mother Nature. Mothers and babies are left together, and herd enclosures are spacious and spattered with shady copses for the herds to nestle in and do deer things. An organic approach fits with the leafy ambience of the valley.

After four years hidden away in the hills, this displaced Englishman has nourished the Pohangina herds of pureblood hinds and stags into some of the tenderest young venison in New Zealand. There are only a select few establishments where Pohangina Valley venison cuts end up on the menu, and much to Her Majesty's chagrin, Buckingham Palace didn't make the list.

Pastry became an obsession for me while working in the pâtisserie at Le Gavroche, London. After years of working in the hot kitchen, the preciseness of the pâtisserie dishes blew me away. It was like working in a laboratory — the chaos and speed of the hot kitchen were left at the door.

Desserts have their rightful place on any menu, anywhere. It's the last thing guests will look at and taste. My philosophy is to keep it simple and keep it seasonal — there's no point serving a strawberry tart in winter, it will be tasteless and will probably cost a fortune.

Final Flings

Dark Chocolate Mousse with Black Cherries — Zibibbo, Wellington

Classic Tiramisu with Hazelnut and Cinnamon Biscotti — Zibibbo, Wellington

Vanilla-bean Pannacotta with Summer Berry Soup — Le Gavroche, London

Pecan and Manuka Honey Tart with Toffee Sauce — Zibibbo, Wellington

Pavlova with Lemon and Paeroa Sorbet — Icon, Wellington

Arlequin of Dark and White Chocolate with Orange Sauce — Le Gavroche, London

Papillote of Summer Fruits with Vanilla-bean Icecream — Fulham Road Restaurant, London

Rhubarb Financiers with Chantilly Cream — The Point, New York

White Chocolate and Mandarin Soup with Spiced Bread — Fulham Road Restaurant, London

Summer Pudding with Clotted Cream — 2 Torr View, Lower Tremar, St. Cleer, Cornwall

Vanilla Shortbread with Spiced Poached Pears — The Heights Restaurant, London

Dark Chocolate Mousse with Black Cherries

The trick to making anything with chocolate is that the end product has to taste of chocolate. Don't overpower it with strong flavours; combinations like chocolate and cherries, or chocolate and orange work well. I prefer to use Otago black cherries. However, cherries are a seasonal item, so if they are hard to find, the poached tinned variety are nearly as good. This recipe is for individual portions, but you can also make it as one large chocolate mousse, using a large dish instead of individual rings.

---

230 ml milk

230 g dark chocolate

100 g butter

4 drops vanilla essence

rum to taste

6 egg yolks

6 egg whites

80 g castor sugar

200 ml cream

75 g pitted black cherries

100 ml whipped cream to garnish

amaretti biscuits to garnish

Boil the milk, then pour into a bowl with the chocolate, butter, vanilla essence and rum. Cover with plastic wrap and place on top of a saucepan of simmering water. Leave on top of the saucepan until the butter and chocolate have melted. Remove from the heat, add egg yolks, and beat with a wooden spoon until smooth. Cover with plastic wrap and allow to cool to room temperature.

Whisk the egg whites for a couple of minutes on high speed, then add the sugar slowly, continuing to whisk until smooth. Do not over-whisk the egg whites as it will make the mousse grainy.

Half whip the 200 ml of cream, until it looks like the thickness of hollandaise sauce. To test, make a figure eight with your whisk, it should disappear after about 8 to 10 seconds. Fold the cream into the chocolate mixture very gently with a spatula.

Place six metal rings about 7.5 cm in diameter on a tray. Place black cherries in the bottom of the rings. Pour in the chocolate mixture, and gently smooth to a flat surface. Refrigerate to set.

To serve

To remove the mousse from the metal rings, rub the outside of the rings with a hot towel (or use a brûlée torch) to slightly melt the chocolate. Carefully remove. Garnish with whipped cream and amaretti biscuits. If you used tinned cherries, you can reduce the syrup from the tin and serve it with the mousse.

Serves 6

Classic Tiramisu with Hazelnut and Cinnamon Biscotti

This classic Italian dessert has made a huge comeback over the past couple of years, popping up on restaurant menus everywhere. The key to this dish is not to be stingy with the Marsala-soaked sponges, and don't use too much cream, as that will make the dish heavy. Tiramisu needs very little garnish. The biscotti can be made in advance and kept in an airtight jar (they're also great with coffee). They are perfect to scoop out the tiramisu with, instead of using a spoon.

450 g mascarpone

4 tablespoons icing sugar

30 ml Marsala

4 egg yolks

4 egg whites

18 ladies finger sponge biscuits
  (see Basics, or you can use the
  packet variety)

200 ml espresso coffee, mixed
  with 30 ml dark rum and
  60 ml brandy

cocoa powder to garnish

hazelnut and cinnamon biscotti
  (see Petits Fours)

Mix together the mascarpone, sugar, Marsala and egg yolks until smooth. Whisk the egg white until it forms firm peaks, then carefully fold into the mascarpone mix.

Place one-third of the sponge fingers in the bottom of a dish and pour over one-third of the coffee mixture. Carefully top with one-third of the mascarpone mix, and repeat until there are 3 layers of sponge fingers and mascarpone. Refrigerate to set.

To serve

Dust with cocoa powder and serve with biscotti. Tiramisu also goes well accompanied by a shot of amaretto on ice.

Serves 6

Vanilla-bean Pannacotta with Summer Berry Soup

Pannacotta seems to have reached cult status in restaurants the world over, replacing lemon tart in the popularity stakes. I first saw this vanilla pannacotta made at Le Gavroche. It was served with an unbelievable selection of poached fruits. Here I have served it only with poached red fruit. This dish is perfect for a light dessert after a summer meal. Be careful with the gelatine though — too much and it will resemble a squash ball. It's tempting to add a little more for safety, but have faith in the quantities given here.

---

1 litre cream

100 g castor sugar

30 ml dark rum

2 vanilla pods

20 g powder gelatine soaked in

   10 ml water

Boil the cream, sugar and rum. Split the 2 vanilla pods down the middle to let all the beans escape, and add the whole pods and the beans to the cream. Cook on low heat, stirring for 2 minutes, allowing the flavours to infuse.

Remove from the heat and mix in the gelatine. Immediately pass through a fine sieve. This needs to be done while the cream is hot.

Ladle into 6 plastic moulds, being sure to stir the mix to get vanilla seeds in each one. Allow to set in the fridge. This should take about 6 hours.

Run the outside of each mould under hot water, then gently ease each pannacotta out of the mould using your finger to create a vacuum on one side.

SUMMER BERRY SOUP

750 ml chardonnay

300 g castor sugar

1 split vanilla pod

juice of 1 lemon

1 punnet hulled strawberries

1 punnet raspberries

1 punnet blueberries

1 punnet blackberries

Bring the chardonnay, sugar, vanilla pod and lemon juice to the boil. Add strawberries, bring back to the boil, then immediately remove from the heat — they will continue to cook enough without direct heat.

Add all the other fruit and pour into a clean bowl, cover with plastic wrap and refrigerate until chilled. The chardonnay liquid will turn a beautiful shade of red. Remove the vanilla pod before serving.

To serve

Place each pannacotta in a soup bowl, pour in some summer berries and a good dash of the chilled poaching liquid, the 'soup'.

Serves 6

Pecan and Manuka Honey Tart with Toffee Sauce

This dessert is pure indulgence; toffee and nuts is a great combination. The beauty of the dish is how all the sugary ingredients really work together. If you don't have a sweet tooth, turn the page.

butter or non-stick spray to grease

450 g sweet pastry (see Basics),
   rolled and cut into 6 discs, each
    12.5 cm diameter

baking beans (e.g. haricot or lima)
   for blind baking

100 g castor sugar

100 g brown sugar

1 tablespoon corn syrup

50 g butter

1 tablespoon manuka honey

1 vanilla pod

splash of brandy

2 cups pecans, toasted for 10
   minutes at 180°C

2 eggs

1 egg yolk

125 ml cream

vanilla icecream to serve

TOFFEE SAUCE

1 cup castor sugar

1 tablespoon water

1 tablespoon butter

¾ cup cream

Grease 6 small baking tins with butter or non-stick spray, and line the bottom and sides with sweet pastry. Place a small piece of baking paper in each tin on top of the pastry and fill each with a handful of baking beans to weigh the pastry down and stop it from rising. Bake for 10–15 minutes at 160°C, or until the pastry is just starting to firm up. Remove the beans and paper and discard them.

Bring the castor sugar, brown sugar, corn syrup, butter, honey, vanilla pod and brandy to the boil in a large saucepan. Remove from the heat and allow to cool to room temperature.

Roughly chop 1½ cups of pecans. Stir the eggs, egg yolk, cream and chopped pecans into the sugar mix. Spoon this mix into the pastry cases, to just below the top. Top with the remaining pecans and bake at 150°C for 1 hour.

For the toffee sauce, bring the sugar and water to the boil and cook until it reaches 140°C or until golden brown. Add the butter and allow it to dissolve in the sugar.

Remove from the heat and add the cream. Whisk to incorporate well. If the mix isn't smooth, return it to a low heat to smooth it out. Strain through a fine sieve and keep at room temperature until ready to serve.

To serve

Spoon toffee sauce onto 6 serving plates. Remove tarts from the tins, and place on top of the toffee sauce. Serve with a scoop of vanilla icecream.

Makes 6 tarts

Pavlova with Lemon and Paeroa Sorbet

This recipe is a bit of fun with two Kiwi classics. I first tried Lemon and Paeroa soft drink (L&P) when I arrived in New Zealand. I experimented with the new flavour and came up with L&P Sorbet. Pavlova seemed like a natural accompaniment. The citrus and sweetness of the sorbet goes really well with the richness of the meringue. I'm not sure if you can buy L&P outside New Zealand. If you can't find L&P, substitute with 7 Up.

PAVLOVA

10 egg whites

½ teaspoon salt

½ teaspoon white vinegar

540 g castor sugar

2 teaspoons cornflour

1 teaspoon vanilla essence

1 cup cream

1 teaspoon icing sugar

cocoa powder to garnish

kiwifruit, peeled and chopped
  to garnish

Combine egg whites, salt and vinegar in a mixer and whisk until it forms soft peaks. Continue mixing and gradually add the castor sugar, little by little, until it forms stiff peaks. Add the cornflour and vanilla essence and mix lightly.

Divide the mixture into 18 and spoon onto an oven tray lined with baking paper. Try to spoon each dollop in the shape of a cookie.

Bake at 110° C for 45 minutes. Turn the oven off and allow to cool in the oven.

In a mixer, whisk the cream and icing sugar until it forms firm peaks.

LEMON AND PAEROA SORBET

600 ml Lemon and Paeroa soft
  drink (L&P)

juice of 1 lemon

90 g corn syrup

250 ml sugar syrup (see Basics)

Mix all ingredients together and churn in an icecream machine to manufacturer's instructions. If you don't have an icecream machine, place all ingredients in a metal bowl and place in the freezer, whisking every 30 minutes until set.

To serve

Place a pavlova disc on each of 6 plates, top with a teaspoon of whipped cream, followed by another pavlova disc. Continue until all the pavlovas are used. Dust the top disc with cocoa powder. Place a scoop of sorbet alongside the pavlova stack and garnish the plate with kiwifruit.

Serves 6

Arlequin of Dark and White Chocolate with Orange Sauce

This dessert is a Le Gavroche classic. It's a decadent chocolate mousse, using the classic combination of chocolate and orange. Use Valrhona extra bitter chocolate if you can find it — the quality really makes a difference.

PASTRY CREAM

12 egg yolks

250 g castor sugar

100 g all-purpose flour

1 litre milk

1 vanilla pod, split

Mix the egg yolks, sugar and flour together. Boil the milk with the split vanilla pod. Pour the hot milk into the egg mixture, mix thoroughly with a wooden spoon and return to a clean saucepan. Continue to cook over low heat, stirring gently. When the mixture starts to thicken and almost boils, remove from the heat and pass through a fine sieve.

DARK AND WHITE CHOCOLATE MOUSSE

200 g dark chocolate

200 g white chocolate

1 litre cream, half whipped

1 quantity sponge biscuits (see Basics), cut into 12 discs each 7.5 cm in diameter before baking

100 g toasted coconut

50 ml dark rum

chocolate shavings to garnish

Melt the dark chocolate and white chocolate in separate bowls. Add half the warm pastry cream to each bowl of chocolate. Mix until completely smooth and allow to cool. When cool, add half the whipped cream to each chocolate mixture. These are the white and dark chocolate mousses.

Place 6 metal rings about 7.5 cm in diameter on a tray. Place a sponge disc in the bottom of each ring. Sprinkle with coconut and drizzle with rum. Pour in the dark chocolate mousse to halfway up each ring. Add another sponge disc. Top with the white chocolate mousse. Allow to set in the fridge.

Once set, remove from the rings by sliding a warm knife around the sides of the ring, or by rubbing the outside with a hot towel to slightly melt the chocolate.

ORANGE SAUCE

½ litre orange juice

100 g castor sugar

1 teaspoon vanilla essence

1 shot Grand Marnier

juice and zest of 4 oranges

Place all the ingredients in a saucepan. Simmer and reduce until it coats the back of a spoon.

Pass through a fine sieve and allow to cool in the fridge.

To serve

Remove arlequins from the moulds and place in the centre of 6 plates. Garnish with orange sauce and chocolate shavings.

Makes 6

Papillote of Summer Fruits with Vanilla-bean Icecream

It is normally fish that is cooked 'en papillote', or in a paper bag. It's a great way to seal in all the flavours of spices and herbs. This recipe uses the same method but here it is fruit and spices that steam in the paper bags as they're baked. This is a popular summer dessert at Zibibbo. The smell of fruit is infectious; once one is ordered and the bag opened in the restaurant, we take orders for them all night. Although the fruits here are summer ones, this recipe also works well with mixed winter fruits.

six 30-cm lengths of tinfoil

six 30-cm lengths of baking paper

2 cups mixed berries

2 peaches

2 nectarines

2 apricots

2 kiwifruit

½ pineapple

2 pears

2 mangoes

6 star anise

6 cinnamon quills

6 cloves

6 ladies finger sponge biscuits (see Basics)

3 cups sugar syrup (see Basics)

1 cup white wine

vanilla-bean icecream (see Basics) to serve

To make each bag for the papillote, place one piece of baking paper on top of a piece of tinfoil, and cut a large circle. This is the bag that will be folded around the fruit.

Remove stones from the stone-fruit, cut all the fruit except the berries into wedges, mix the chopped fruit together with the berries and divide the fruit among 6 bags. Place one piece of each of the spices and one sponge finger in each bag. Fold each bag in half to make a half-moon shape. Fold the edges over twice to seal, leaving a 2.5-cm gap at one end.

Mix the sugar syrup and white wine together. Pour about half a cup into each bag and fold to seal the end.

Place the bags on an oven tray and bake at 250° C for 12–15 minutes.

To serve

Remove from the oven and serve the bags immediately at the table on hot plates. Serve with vanilla-bean icecream. The best way to eat these is to cut a hole in the bag and throw the icecream in to melt through the fruit.

Serves 6

Rhubarb Financiers with Chantilly Cream

Financier is a type of cake made with lots of butter. It's best served warm with whipped or pouring cream. The rhubarb will work its way through the cake during cooking.

6 egg whites

150 g icing sugar

75 g ground almonds

50 g all-purpose flour

grated zest of 2 lemons

125 g butter

seeds from 1 vanilla pod

2 sticks of rhubarb, peeled

1 cup sugar syrup

butter or non-stick spray to grease

Beat together the egg whites, icing sugar, ground almonds and flour until really smooth. Add the lemon zest.

In a small saucepan, melt the butter and add the vanilla pod seeds. Cook until the butter is light brown and nutty smelling. Allow to cool. Fold the butter and vanilla seeds into the egg mixture. Allow to rest for about 10 minutes.

Cut the rhubarb into 2-cm-long pieces and cook on low heat in the sugar syrup for 10 minutes. Drain and allow to cool.

Grease 6 ceramic moulds with butter or non-stick spray. Place a couple of pieces of rhubarb in the bottom of each, reserving some rhubarb to use as a garnish. Spoon over the egg mixture to 1 cm below the top of the moulds.

Bake at 150° C for 40 minutes, then remove from the oven and allow to rest for 10 minutes.

CHANTILLY CREAM

1 cup cream

a few drops of vanilla essence or
    the seeds from one vanilla pod

1 tablespoon sifted icing sugar

Mix all the ingredients together. Whisk until thickened.

To serve

Turn the financiers out onto 6 serving plates. Spoon on a good dollop of chantilly cream, and garnish with the cooked rhubarb.

Serves 6

White Chocolate and Mandarin Soup with Spiced Bread

This dessert is fluffy, light and very rich. The bread is cooked like French toast and the dish is topped with vanilla-bean icecream. The smooth richness of the chocolate goes really well with the spicy bread.

---

250 g white chocolate

½ cup sugar syrup (see Basics)

1 shot amaretto

4 egg yolks

zest and juice of 2 mandarins

1 shot of mandarin brandy or

    Cointreau

150 ml cream

1 tablespoon icing sugar

seeds from 1 vanilla pod

6 scoops vanilla-bean icecream

    (see Basics)

Melt the chocolate in a bowl over a saucepan of boiling water. Set aside.

In another bowl, mix the sugar syrup, amaretto and egg yolks. Cook over a saucepan of boiling water, stirring constantly, until fluffy.

Remove from the heat and allow to cool for a couple of minutes, then fold into the melted chocolate. Add the mandarin juice and zest and the mandarin brandy.

Half whip the cream with the icing sugar and vanilla pod seeds. When the chocolate mixture is cool, add the whipped cream. Cover with plastic wrap and set aside.

SPICED BREAD

1 whole egg

1 cup cream

2 tablespoons sifted icing sugar

6 slices of spiced bread

2 tablespoons butter

Mix the egg with the cream and icing sugar. Dip each piece of bread in the mixture and fry in the butter in a non-stick frying pan until golden brown.

To serve

Take 6 serving bowls and place a piece of bread in the bottom of each. Pour over the chocolate mandarin soup mix and glaze under a medium-hot grill until golden brown. Garnish with a scoop of vanilla-bean icecream.

Serves 6

Summer Pudding with Clotted Cream

I love the simplicity of this classic English dessert. There's nothing better than red fruit when it's at its best in the middle of summer. The sugar content of red fruit does vary, so adjust the sugar to taste. I've served the pudding here with clotted cream, but icecream is just as good.

1 punnet strawberries

1 punnet raspberries

1 punnet blueberries

1 punnet blackberries

250 g castor sugar

zest and juice of 1 lemon

12 slices fresh white bread, crusts
 removed

selection of fresh berries to
 garnish

1 punnet clotted cream to garnish

Place all the fruit, with the sugar, lemon zest and lemon juice in a thick-bottomed saucepan. Cook until the fruit is soft (about 10–15 minutes). Test to see if it is sweet enough and add more sugar if required. Strain the fruit and allow to cool. Keep both the fruit and the juice.

Place 6 rings about 4 cm in diameter on a tray. Line the bottom of each ring with one slice of bread. Pour the fruit into the bread-lined rings and add a little of the juice. Cover the tops with bread slices. Use a heavy weight to cover the top of all the rings. This will press the fruit and bread together. Some juice will be pressed out, so keep this juice for serving with the pudding. Refrigerate for at least 6 hours.

To serve

Remove the puddings from the moulds and place each one in the centre of a serving plate. Garnish with a selection of fresh berries, and a big spoonful of clotted cream.

Serves 6

Vanilla Shortbread with Spiced Poached Pears

Pears and chocolate are made for each other. In this recipe pears are combined with white chocolate icecream, and served with vanilla shortbread.

SHORTBREAD

500 g unsalted butter

540 g sifted icing sugar

750 g all-purpose flour

4 drops vanilla essence

1 pinch salt

6 egg yolks

75 ml cream

icing sugar for dusting

Mix the butter and sugar in a mixer on the lowest speed until smooth. Add the flour, vanilla essence and salt. With the mixer still running, add the egg yolks one at a time until fully mixed in. Add the cream slowly and continue to mix until smooth. Remove the shortbread paste from the mixer and refrigerate until cool.

Roll the paste out on a floured bench, to just over ½ cm thick and cut out with a large crinkle-shaped cutter. Place on a tray covered with baking paper and leave to rest for 5 minutes. Bake at 150°C for 15 minutes. Remove and cool on baking rack. Dust with icing sugar.

POACHED PEARS

500 ml water

150 g castor sugar

2 star anise

1 cinnamon stick

3 cloves

2 lemons, cut in half

1 lime, cut in half

6 pears, peeled and cored

castor sugar for dusting

Bring the water, sugar and spices to the boil. Add the lemon and lime halves. Reduce the heat to a simmer and add the pears whole. Poach the pears until tender, about 20 minutes, and then allow to cool in the cooking liquid at room temperature.

Cut each pear into six or eight segments, but leave the last centimetre of each segment at the narow end uncut so the pear holds together. Dust with castor sugar and glaze with a brûlée torch or by baking in a hot oven.

WHITE CHOCOLATE ICECREAM GARNISH

**12 thin pear slices, cut with a
   sharp knife**

icing sugar for dusting

6 scoops white chocolate icecream

Dust the pear slices with icing sugar and bake at 180° C for 5 minutes or until crisp. Sandwich a scoop of icecream between two slices of crisp pear.

To serve

Place one pear on each piece of shortbread, alongside the white chocolate icecream garnish.

Serves 6

THE TEAM

One thing I've learnt from all the chefs that have motivated me throughout my career is that if you have no teamwork, you have nothing.

The raw energy that can be created by team members all working towards the same end is incredible. When the kitchen is working as a team, and the kitchen and restaurant are working together as a team, I know this will flow through to ensure that the customer has a great experience. Remember, though, that all the best teams have leaders with the vision and the courage to say what they think at the right time. All teams need both superstars and muppets to make them work.

As a head chef it's important to step up to the crease and lead by example when the service or the night is not going so well. I look at the leaders of the great kitchens of the world in the same light as the great leaders of sports teams; the rest of the team need someone they can believe in to get them through the hard times.

At Zibibbo we create a working environment where all the staff are important, they all have their place and know exactly what we require of them at the right time. Staff who don't come up to scratch or who have a problem getting on with people usually leave quickly enough. The staff who share the vision of teamwork and excellence stay with us a long time.

Some people would say preparing petits fours is a donkey job, but it's actually a job that takes a great deal of skill and concentration. Petits fours became an obsession for me when I worked in the pâtisserie at Le Gavroche. Michel Roux Jnr placed an incredible amount of importance on petits fours, because this would be the last morsel of food that the customers would eat before leaving the restaurant. One chef would start at 5 am and work a solid 12 hours to prepare the petits fours. To see all the petits fours placed on the silver stands before service was a Kodak moment.

Petits Fours

Almond and Orange Wafers — Le Gavroche, London

Hazelnut and Cinnamon Biscotti — Zibibbo, Wellington

Blueberry Financiers — The Point, New York

Vanilla-bean Shortbread with Lemon Curd — Zibibbo, Wellington

Apple Madeleines — The Point, New York

Jammy Dodgers — Fulham Road Restaurant, London

Nougat — Le Gavroche, London

Whisky Truffles — Fulham Road Restaurant, London

Jaffa Cakes — The Heights, London

Coconut and Chocolate Crunch — The Heights, London

Dark Chocolate and Pecan Nut Slab — The Point, New York

Almond and Orange Wafers

The mix for these wafers is very easy to make. But be careful with them once they're cooked, because they'll be very delicate. The beauty of these wafers is their crunchiness.

---

375 g unsalted butter, softened

375 g castor sugar

5 eggs, beaten

375 g sifted all-purpose flour

375 g ground almonds

juice and zest of 2 oranges

200 g chopped almonds

Pre-heat oven to 160° C.

Cream the butter and sugar in a bowl. Continue to mix, and slowly add the beaten eggs. Mix the sifted flour and ground almonds together and add to the mixture. Mix to a smooth paste. Add the orange juice, zest and chopped almonds, and mix again until smooth. Refrigerate for at least 2 hours before using.

Line a baking tray with paper and spread the mixture onto the tray, smoothing it into circles with a palette knife. The best way to get a neat round circle is to cut one out of an icecream container, then place the container with the hole in it on the baking tray and fill in the hole with the wafer mix, smoothing it over with the palette knife. When you have a dozen circles, bake at 160° C for 10–12 minutes until evenly golden brown.

At Zibibbo we have a wafer tray to cool the wafers on, but you can use a rolling pin. Drape the warm wafers over it, allowing them to cool in a nice half-moon shape.

Makes 24

Clockwise from top: Coconut and Chocolate Crunch, Apple Madeleines, Jaffa Cakes, Vanilla-bean Shortbread with Lemon Curd, Hazelnut and Cinnamon Biscotti, Whisky Truffles, Nougat, Jammy Dodgers, Almond and Orange Wafers, Dark Chocolate and Pecan Nut Slab, Blueberry Financiers.

Hazelnut and Cinnamon Biscotti

This recipe uses hazelnuts, but you can add any type of nuts or dried fruit. Walnuts and dried apricots work really well.

150 g castor sugar

150 g plain flour, sifted

½ teaspoon vanilla essence

2 teaspoons baking powder

2 eggs

½ teaspoon ground cinnamon

½ cup roasted peeled hazelnuts

Place all ingredients in a bowl and mix well. Spoon mixture onto an oven tray lined with baking paper, in a log shape 2 cm wide. The logs will droop a little, but that doesn't matter. Bake at 160° C for 20 minutes or until set. Allow to cool.

Using a bread knife, slice the biscotti log into ½-cm slices. Remove the baking paper from the tray and place the slices down flat back on the baking tray.

Put back into the oven, and bake for 10 minutes at 120° C.

Makes 12 large biscotti

Blueberry Financiers

These buttery little cakes are given a bite by the addition of blueberries, which are full of flavour and very juicy. You can also use any other fruit. Apricots work really well. The financiers are best eaten on the day they're baked.

1 egg white

2 egg yolks

50 g icing sugar, sieved

15 g all-purpose flour

20 g ground almonds

1 teaspoon lemon zest

4 drops vanilla essence

45 g unsalted butter

1 punnet fresh blueberries

Cream the egg white, egg yolks, icing sugar, flour and ground almonds until smooth. Fold in the lemon zest and vanilla essence.

Cook the butter on a low heat until it is golden brown and smells nutty. Allow the butter to cool, then fold it into the mixture.

Pipe the mix into 12 small muffin tins and stud with blueberries. Bake at 150° C for 35 minutes. Remove and place on cooking wire.

Makes 12

Vanilla-bean Shortbread with Lemon Curd

Blending the whole vanilla pod with sugar gives this shortbread a far better flavour than normal shortbread. The shortbreads can be eaten plain or with the lemon curd, and if you have any lemon curd left over, it's great on toast.

---

170 g icing sugar

1 vanilla pod

180 g unsalted butter, softened

240 g all-purpose flour

120 g cornflour

4 drops vanilla essence

50 ml cold milk

icing sugar for dusting

castor sugar

Pre-heat oven to 150° C.

Place the icing sugar and whole vanilla pod in a food processor and blend until the pod is like powder. Add the softened butter and mix until smooth. With the mixer still on, add the flour, cornflour and vanilla essence. Slowly add the cold milk and mix until smooth.

Remove from the mixer and wrap in plastic wrap. Refrigerate for a couple of hours to cool.

Dust the bench with icing sugar and roll the dough to just over 1 cm thick. Cut with a medium-sized cutter. Place on a greased tray and rest for 5 minutes.

Sprinkle the shortbread with castor sugar and bake for 15 minutes at 150° C.

Makes 24 medium-sized biscuits

LEMON CURD

4 egg yolks

50 g castor sugar

25 g butter

zest of 2 lemons

juice of 3 lemons

pistachios or almonds to garnish

Mix the egg yolks and sugar in a stainless steel bowl until smooth. Add all the other ingredients, except the nuts, and mix again until smooth.

Place the mixture over a saucepan of simmering water and cook over a medium heat, stirring constantly. When the egg yolks start to cook, the curd will thicken like mayonnaise. Don't let the mixture boil, or it will curdle. Remove from the heat and pass through a fine sieve. Leave to cool.

Spread the mixture over the cooked shortbread with a palette knife. Garnish with a few chopped pistachios or almonds.

Apple Madeleines

These tiny apple cakes are great with coffee. In France, madeleines are baked in small fluted tins, also called 'madeleines', but small muffin tins work just as well. Madeleines are best served on the day they're made.

2 eggs

75 g castor sugar

10 g brown sugar

3 drops vanilla essence

100 g all-purpose flour

1 teaspoon baking powder

100 g clear honey

100 g melted butter

100 g Granny Smith apples,
   finely diced

unsalted butter or non-stick spray
   to grease

icing sugar to garnish

Cream the eggs, castor sugar, brown sugar and vanilla essence in a mixer. Fold in the flour and baking powder with a spatula. Melt the honey and butter together and add to the mixture. Fold in the diced apple.

Pour the mix halfway up greased madeleines or mini muffin tins and bake at 160° C for 25 minutes.

Remove from tins and cool on cooling wire. Dust with icing sugar and serve.

Makes 12 small madeleines

Jammy Dodgers

This is a take on the classic British Jammy Dodger biscuit. I use strawberry jam in the recipe, but any red fruit jam works well.

---

170 g icing sugar

1 vanilla pod

180 g unsalted butter, softened

240 g all-purpose flour

120 g cornflour

4 drops vanilla essence

50 ml cold milk

75 g strawberry jam

icing sugar to garnish

Pre-heat oven to 160° C.

Place the icing sugar and whole vanilla pod in a food processor and blend until the pod is like powder. Add the softened butter and mix until smooth. With the mixer still on, add the flour, cornflour and vanilla essence. Slowly add the cold milk and again mix until smooth.

Remove from the mixer and wrap in plastic wrap. Refrigerate for a couple of hours to cool.

Dust the bench with icing sugar and roll the dough to just over 1 cm thick. Cut 24 round disc shapes with a cutter. Cut a smaller heart shape out of the centre of 12 of these discs with another cutter. Place the shapes on a greased tray and sprinkle with castor sugar. Bake for 12–15 minutes at 160° C.

Allow to cool, then spread a little of the jam on each round disc and top with the discs that have the heart shapes cut out of them. Dust with icing sugar and serve.

Makes 12

Nougat

Making nougat reminds me of the days when my grandmother would take me to the sweetshop to buy it in big slabs. Nougat is a challenge to master, but once you get your head around the timing of all the ingredients, it is really easy. A warning, though: be prepared to get sticky! You'll need a sugar thermometer for this recipe.

310 g castor sugar

100 ml water

80 g corn syrup

1 egg white

pinch of castor sugar

100 g clear honey, warmed

100 g peeled roast hazelnuts

120 g roast almonds

30 g peeled pistachios

80 g diced dried apricots

20 g glacé cherries

icing sugar to dust

Heat the castor sugar, water and corn syrup in a thick-bottom saucepan until it reaches 120°C on the sugar thermometer. When the syrup gets to 120°C, start whisking the egg white in a mixer with a pinch of sugar, until it forms soft peaks. You'll need a good quality mixer for this.

When the syrup reaches 145°C, it will be slightly caramelised. Remove it from the heat and slowly pour the caramel into the whisked egg whites. After the caramel is added, slowly add the warm honey. Leave this in the mixer on the lowest speed for 20 minutes to cool.

Add the fruit and nuts. Then (this is where the sticky part begins), spread the mixture with a spatula onto trays dusted with icing sugar.

Allow one day to set at room temperature. Cut the nougat into cubes with a very sharp knife. Dust with icing sugar and serve.

Makes 1 tray

Whisky Truffles

These truffles are so easy to make and they are a great way to finish a meal. You can substitute the whisky for your favourite liquor. Cointreau goes really well — the old chocolate and orange combination. At Zibibbo, we serve these truffles with coffee at Christmas time.

100 ml cream

360 g dark chocolate

100 g icing sugar, sieved

60 ml whisky, warmed

100 g cocoa powder

Boil the cream, remove from heat and add the chocolate broken into chunks. Whisk until smooth, then whisk in the sieved icing sugar. Pour in the warmed whisky and whisk again until smooth.

Remove from the saucepan and place on a tray that has been covered with baking paper. Cover with plastic wrap, and place in the fridge to set.

When the mixture is set, divide into 20 equal portions and roll into balls in the palm of your hand. Roll the balls in cocoa powder and reset in the fridge.

Makes 20 truffles

Jaffa Cakes

I used to love eating these in England when I was a child. The chocolate and orange flavour combination is great. Choose a tangy marmalade for the filling.

100 ml cream

100 g dark chocolate

2 tablespoons orange marmalade

24 sponge discs 5 cm in diameter, cut from sponge biscuits (see Basics)

Boil the cream and remove from heat. Melt the chocolate in the cream. Allow to cool for 20 minutes, then mix with a spatula until smooth. If the mix starts getting too thick, return to the heat and it will soften up. Squash a small amount of marmalade between 2 sponge discs to make a sandwich. Repeat with the other discs. Half dip one side of each sandwich into the warm chocolate and place on a tray to set.

Makes 12

Coconut and Chocolate Crunch

This has the flavour of a Bounty Bar — chocolate and coconut. I've also included cherries for added flavour and texture.

200 g dark chocolate

100 g unsalted butter

350 g sweetened condensed milk

250 g toasted grated coconut

200 g dried glacé cherries,
   chopped

Melt the chocolate and butter in a bowl over a saucepan of boiling water. Fold all the other ingredients into the chocolate and mix until smooth.

Cover a tray with edges in baking paper and spread the mixture on with a spatula. Allow to set in the fridge. Remove from the tray and cut into bite-size pieces.

Serves 12

Dark Chocolate and Pecan Nut Slab

This is an easy recipe, but one with interesting flavours that will have your guests trying to guess what's in it. I've used pecans, but any type of nut will work.

200 g dark chocolate

100 g unsalted butter

300 g sweetened condensed milk

150 g crushed gingernuts

300 g chopped dried apricots

200 g chopped pecan nuts

Melt chocolate and butter in separate bowls, then combine. Fold all the other ingredients into the chocolate and mix until smooth.

Take a medium-sized baking tray that has a raised edge and line it in baking paper. Spread the mixture on 2 cm thick with a spatula. Allow to set in the fridge. Remove from tray and cut into bite-size pieces.

Serves 12

The recipes in this section are the 'building blocks' which have to be perfected first. How can you build the Empire State Building if you have no idea how to mix concrete? It's as simple as that!

All the new chefs at Zibibbo are first put on one day's trial and given all the basic jobs to complete, starting with cutting up vegetables and then moving on to some of the recipes in this section. This method of interviewing is a good way to see if someone will cut the mustard or not. It also makes the new chefs at Zibibbo understand that the basics are the most important thing they need to learn and perfect before moving on to the more difficult side of cooking.

All the basic recipes in this section can be used for the relevant recipes in the book or kept for use later on with other dishes.

Basics

Lemon and Rosemary Butter	Tomato Fondue	Herb Gnocchi
Garlic Butter	Balsamic Vinegar Reduction	Pasta Dough
Beurre Blanc	Romesco Sauce	Puff Pastry
Mayonnaise	Kalamata Black Olive Sauce	Sweet Pastry
Aïoli	Quick Tomato and Basil Sauce	Homemade Ricotta Cheese
Saffron Aïoli	Red Wine Sauce	Preserved Lemons
Rouille	Lamb Sauce	Sugar Syrup
Basil Oil	Duck Sauce	Hokey Pokey
Rocket or Basil Pesto	Onion Gravy	Vanilla-bean Icecream
Tzatziki	Chicken Stock	Crostini
Salsa Verde	Beef Stock	Sponge Biscuits (Ladies Fingers)
	Fish Stock	

Lemon and Rosemary Butter

200 g salted butter, softened
1 red onion, diced
1 medium-hot red chilli, seeds discarded and
 chopped
leaves from 1 rosemary sprig, chopped
½ cup chopped flat-leaf parsley
juice and zest of 2 limes
juice and zest of 2 lemons
salt and pepper

Place the butter in a bowl and mix with all the other
ingredients. Season with salt and pepper. Leave at room
temperature.

Garlic Butter

500 g salted butter, softened
500 ml extra virgin olive oil
1 bunch flat-leaf parsley
10 cloves garlic, peeled
salt and pepper

Place all ingredients in a food processor and pulse until
combined well and parsley is chopped. Remove and
refrigerate in a container with a good seal. Use as
required. This will keep for several weeks in the fridge.

Beurre Blanc

250 ml white wine
½ cup chopped shallots
250 ml cream
100 g cold butter, cut into cubes
2 tablespoons chives, chopped
salt and pepper

Cook the wine and shallots in a small saucepan on
medium heat until the wine is almost completely
evaporated. Add the cream and reduce by half.

Remove from the heat and whisk in the butter, one
cube at a time. Continue whisking while adding the
butter or it will separate from the sauce. Strain the
sauce through a sieve and mix in the chives. Season
with salt and pepper.

This sauce is best served straight away, but can be
gently reheated on low heat, continually whisking until
hot. Do not boil.

Mayonnaise

4 egg yolks
1 tablespoon Dijon mustard
juice of 1 lemon
1½ cups olive oil
salt and pepper

Blend the egg yolks, mustard and lemon juice in a food
processor on high speed for 1 minute. With the motor
running, gradually add the olive oil in a thin steady
stream until well incorporated. Season with salt and
pepper. Makes 2 cups.

Aïoli

4 egg yolks
1 tablespoon Dijon mustard
juice of 1 lemon
2 cloves garlic
1½ cups olive oil
salt and pepper

Blend the egg yolks, mustard, lemon juice and garlic in a food processor on high speed for 1 minute. With the motor running, gradually add the olive oil in a thin steady stream until well incorporated. Season with salt and pepper. Makes 2 cups.

Chive variation: Add 3 tablespoons of chopped chives after step 2.

Saffron Aïoli

4 tablespoons white wine vinegar
1 pinch saffron threads
3 egg yolks
1 teaspoon Dijon mustard
½ clove garlic
¾ cup olive oil
salt and pepper

Bring the vinegar and saffron to the boil in a small saucepan. Remove from heat and allow to cool.

Blend the egg yolks, mustard, garlic and saffron-infused vinegar in a food processor for 1 minute. With the motor running, gradually add the olive oil in a thin steady stream until well incorporated. Season with salt and pepper.

Rouille

½ red capsicum
½ teaspoon Dijon mustard
½ teaspoon harissa paste (chilli paste)
10 ml white wine vinegar
4 egg yolks
½ clove chopped garlic
25 g new potatoes, peeled and cooked
100 ml extra virgin olive oil
salt and pepper

Roast the red capsicum at 180° C until soft (about 15 minutes).

Place the mustard, chilli paste and white wine vinegar in a food processor on high speed. Process for 30 seconds. Add the egg yolks and blend for a further 30 seconds. Add the red capsicum, garlic and potatoes and blend for 2 minutes. Pour in the olive oil slowly in a thin steady stream, so it ends up like a mayonnaise. Season with salt and pepper.

Rouille can be stored in an airtight container in the fridge for up to 2 weeks.

Basil Oil

1 cup basil leaves
½ cup flat-leaf parsley
1 cup olive oil

Blend all ingredients in a blender for 3 minutes. Strain the oil mixture through a fine strainer to remove any large pieces of herbs.

Rocket or Basil Pesto

100 g rocket leaves, picked from the stalks and
   washed, or 2 cups fresh basil leaves
¼ cup toasted pine nuts
¼ cup grated parmesan
2 cloves garlic, chopped
2 tablespoons flat-leaf parsley
½ cup extra virgin olive oil
salt and pepper

Place all ingredients in a food processor and blend to
the desired consistency.

Tzatziki

2 telegraph cucumbers, peeled, seeded
   and finely diced
1½ cups good quality Greek yoghurt
2 cloves garlic, chopped
½ cup chopped mint leaves
salt and pepper

Mix cucumber with 1 teaspoon of salt, and allow to sit
for 1 hour. Rinse and dry the cucumber. Mix the
cucumber, yoghurt, garlic and mint until well
combined. Season with salt and pepper.

Salsa Verde

1 cup flat-leaf parsley leaves
1 tablespoon capers
1 tablespoon red wine vinegar
2 anchovy fillets
½ cup mint leaves
1 cup extra virgin olive oil

Place all the ingredients in a blender, and blend on
high speed until a smooth paste. This can be kept in
the fridge for up to a week.

Tomato Fondue

250 g Roma tomatoes
½ small red onion, finely chopped
½ clove garlic, chopped
2 teaspoons thyme leaves
25 g butter
25 ml white wine
2 tablespoons shredded basil leaves
salt and pepper

Blanch the tomatoes in a pot of boiling water for 10
seconds. Remove and plunge into ice water. Peel, cut
into quarters and discard the seeds.

Sauté the red onion, garlic and thyme in butter on low
heat until soft. Add the tomatoes and white wine and
cook until completely soft. Mix in the basil and season
with salt and pepper.

Balsamic Vinegar Reduction

700 ml balsamic vinegar
2 tablespoons brown sugar
1 star anise
1 cinnamon quill

Place all ingredients in a small saucepan. Bring to a simmer on a low heat and reduce until one-third of the liquid remains. Strain through a fine strainer to remove the star anise and cinnamon.

Romesco Sauce

1 red capsicum
1 red onion, chopped
2 medium-hot fresh chillies, seeds discarded
olive oil for roasting
2 Roma tomatoes
4 anchovies
½ cup ground roast almonds
1 tablespoon white wine vinegar
1 cup toasted white bread, crusts removed
½ cup extra virgin olive oil
salt and pepper

Roast the red capsicum, red onion and chillies in a little olive oil on 180° C for 10–15 minutes until soft and caramelised.

Cut the tomatoes in half lengthways and sear in a hot frying pan, flesh side down, for a couple of minutes until blackened.

Place all ingredients except the extra virgin olive oil in a food processor and blend for 2 minutes or until smooth. With the motor running, gradually add the olive oil in a thin steady stream until well incorporated. Season with salt and pepper.

Kalamata Black Olive Sauce

100 g pitted Kalamata olives
juice of 1 lemon
juice of 1 lime
1 clove garlic, chopped
50 g plump anchovy fillets
50 ml extra virgin olive oil

Place all the ingredients in a blender and leave to blend until a fine purée. Remove and strain through a sieve.

Quick Tomato and Basil Sauce

1 white onion, chopped
2 garlic cloves, chopped
1 cup olive oil
pinch dried red chilli flakes
8 Roma tomatoes, chopped
1 tablespoon white sugar
2 cups basil leaves, cut into strips
salt and pepper

Gently fry the onion and garlic in olive oil until soft. Add the chilli flakes and cook until soft. Add the tomatoes and cook for 15 minutes. Add the sugar.

Purée in a blender and pass through a fine sieve. Add the basil leaves and season with salt and pepper.

Red Wine Sauce

2 tablespoons olive oil
500 g braising beef pieces
250 g beefsteak tomatoes, cut in half
1 carrot, peeled and chopped
1 stick celery, peeled and chopped
1 white onion, peeled and chopped
½ leek
½ bottle red wine
3 litres beef stock
½ cup thyme leaves
1 bay leaf
50 ml red wine vinegar

Heat the olive oil in a saucepan on high heat and add the beef pieces. Cook until brown, then remove the beef and set aside.

Put the vegetables in the saucepan and cook until golden brown. Put back the beef, and add the red wine. Allow to reduce until thick and syrupy. Add the stock, thyme, bay leaf and red wine vinegar. Simmer on low heat for 1 hour.

Strain through a fine sieve, then put into a clean saucepan. Reduce by two-thirds on high heat. Strain through a fine sieve again and skim off any fat.

Lamb Sauce

Prepare as for the red wine sauce, but replace beef pieces with lamb pieces.

Duck Sauce

Prepare as for the red wine sauce, but replace beef pieces with duck trimmings.

Onion Gravy

100 g white onion, chopped
10 g garlic, chopped
olive oil for frying
200 ml dry white wine
2 bay leaves
1 litre beef stock
50 g parsley, chopped
salt and pepper

Fry the onion and garlic gently in olive oil without colouring. Add the wine and bay leaves, and simmer for 3 minutes. Add the beef stock and simmer until reduced by about one-third and the sauce is a good consistency. Just before serving, remove the bay leaf and add the parsley. Season with salt and pepper.

Chicken Stock

2 kg chicken bones
1 carrot, peeled and chopped
1 onion, peeled and chopped
2 celery sticks, chopped
½ leek top, chopped
3 sprigs thyme
3 sprigs parsley
2 bay leaves
4 peppercorns
1 star anise

Cover the chicken bones with cold water (the quantity will depend on the size of the saucepan) and slowly bring to a simmer. Skim off the excess fat. Add the vegetables, bring back to simmering point and simmer for a further 5 hours. Add the herbs and spices and simmer for a further hour. At no point should the stock be boiled.

Pass through a fine sieve into a clean saucepan. Return to the heat and skim off the remaining fat.

Beef Stock

2 kg small beef bones
canola oil for roasting
1 chopped carrot
1 chopped onion
2 stalks celery, chopped
cloves from 1 bulb garlic
1 bottle red wine
1 sprig rosemary
3 sprigs thyme
6 chopped Roma tomatoes
cold water

Roast the beef bones in canola oil at 180° C, turning frequently until golden brown. Remove and set aside.

In the same tray, roast the carrot, onion, celery and garlic in canola oil, turning frequently until golden brown. Remove and add to the bones.

Pour off excess oil from the tray and add all the red wine. Scrape all the stuck bits from the tray using a wooden spoon.

Place the bones, vegetables, wine mixture and the remaining ingredients in a large saucepan and cover with cold water (the quantity of water will depend on the size of the saucepan). Slowly bring to a simmer and simmer for 4 hours. Do not boil.

During cooking, scrape off any impurities that rise to the surface.

Strain the stock through a fine sieve and again remove any scum from the surface.

Fish Stock

1 kg bones from white fish
canola oil for frying bones
1 carrot, peeled and chopped
1 white onion, chopped
2 stalks celery, chopped
100 ml white wine
6 peppercorns
6 coriander seeds
2 bay leaves
2 star anise
4 parsley stalks
1.5 litres water

Fry the bones in canola oil in a heavy-bottom frying pan without colouring them. Add the chopped vegetables, white wine, peppercorns and coriander seeds. Cook for 2 minutes on low heat.

Add the bay leaf, star anise, parsley stalks and water. Bring to the boil, then turn down the heat and simmer on low for 20 minutes. Strain through a fine sieve.

Herb Gnocchi

½ kg potato, cooked and mashed
2 egg yolks
½ cup grated parmesan
½ cup chopped parsley
1 bunch chopped chives
salt and pepper
¾ cup all-purpose flour

Mix by hand the potato, egg yolks, parmesan, parsley, chives, salt and pepper. Mix into a smooth ball. Add the flour and knead until smooth. Refrigerate for 30 minutes to rest.

Divide into four, and roll into long snake-like shapes on a floured bench. Cut at an angle across the gnocchi roll, with a sharp knife. To cook, blanch the gnocchi for a couple of minutes in a large saucepan of boiling salted water until cooked. Remove and place in a single layer on a tray brushed with olive oil. Makes 600 g.

Pasta Dough

650 g all-purpose flour
pinch of table salt
4 whole medium-sized eggs
6 egg yolks
50 ml extra virgin olive oil

Place the flour and salt in a food processor on low speed. Pulse the mixture and slowly add the eggs one by one, then the egg yolks. Continue to pulse until the mixture has started to form a ball. Slowly add the olive oil. Pulse for a further 2 minutes.

Remove the mix and knead on a floured bench until smooth. Wrap in plastic wrap and refrigerate for a couple of hours before using.

Puff Pastry

½ kg all-purpose flour
½ tablespoon salt
45 g unsalted butter
200 ml water
160 g butter — cut into one large rectangle,
   1 cm thick

Mix together the flour, salt, 45 g butter and water until extremely smooth and pliable. Knead for 5 minutes, then allow to rest for 30 minutes in the fridge.

Roll out the pastry to about 5 cm thick on a floured bench, trying to keep it a rectangular shape. Place the 160 g rectangle of butter into the centre of the pastry. Fold two sides of the pastry over to meet in the middle, just joining each end. Repeat with the other two sides. This is the first fold. Roll out again to about 5 cm, keeping a rectangle shape. Fold one-third of the pastry on top of the rest of the pastry to halfway, and fold the remaining one-third over the top of this to form a rectangle. This is the second fold. Allow to rest in the fridge for half an hour.

Repeat this process (including refrigerating) 2 more times. Roll out the pastry on a floured bench to the desired thickness and cut to the desired shape.

Sweet Pastry

1 kg all-purpose flour
600 g unsalted butter
400 g sugar
8 eggs

Rub the flour and butter together until it resembles breadcrumbs. Mix in the sugar and eggs and continue to mix until it forms a ball. Knead for 4–5 minutes on a floured bench until smooth. Rest in the fridge for at least 1 hour before using.

Homemade Ricotta Cheese

1 litre milk
125 ml cream
juice of 1 lemon
salt and pepper

Bring the milk and cream to the boil. Remove from heat and add lemon juice.

The mixture will split and the ricotta will rise to the top. Transfer the whole mixture to a bowl and leave overnight in the fridge to completely split. Remove the ricotta (curds) with a slotted spoon and refrigerate until needed.

Preserved Lemons

1 kg lemons
1 cup rock salt
2 cloves
1 cinnamon stick
1 cup lemon juice

Cut 2 short slits into the lemons, one at the top and one at the bottom. Rub rock salt into the slits. Pack well into a sterilised jar, add the spices and leftover salt. Pour over the lemon juice and refrigerate for 2 days.

Fill the jar with water and refrigerate for 1 month.

Sugar Syrup

500 ml water
500 g castor sugar
1 vanilla pod, halved

Place all the ingredients in a saucepan and bring to the boil. Simmer for 1 minute. Strain through a fine sieve and cool.

Hokey Pokey

175 g castor sugar
25 g honey
75 g glucose
30 ml water
1 teaspoon bicarbonate of soda

Bring the sugar, honey, glucose and water to the boil in a high-sided saucepan. Continue to cook until it reaches 140°C or until golden brown.

Add the bicarbonate of soda and quickly mix well. Pour onto a piece of baking paper. Allow to cool before cutting to desired size. It is easiest to use a serrated-edge knife.

Vanilla-bean Icecream

7 medium-sized egg yolks
150 g castor sugar
500 ml milk
4 vanilla pods, split open, or 1 teaspoon vanilla
   essence
150 ml double cream

Mix the egg yolks and sugar together to a smooth paste.

Boil the milk and vanilla pods for two minutes. Scrape vanilla pods with a knife to make sure all the seeds are out but leave them in the milk.

Pour a little of the hot liquid over the egg yolks. Mix well with a spatula. Add the milk in small quantities — if you add all the hot liquid at once, you'll end up with scrambled eggs. Continue mixing and add the rest of the liquid slowly.

Return the mixture to a thick-bottomed saucepan and cook very slowly, stirring all the time until the mixture coats the back of a spoon. Remove from the heat and pass through a fine sieve. Add the double cream and allow to cool.

Place the mixture in an icecream machine and allow to set, churning periodically according to the manufacturer's instructions. If you don't have an icecream machine, place in a bowl in the freezer and stir every ½ hour until the mixture is set. It won't be the same as machine-churned icecream, but it is a good alternative.

Crostini

1 French stick
2 cloves garlic, cut in half
1 tablespoon chopped rosemary
1 tablespoon chopped thyme
1 cup olive oil

Cut the French stick into slices ½ cm thick. Rub with the garlic and sprinkle with the herbs. Bake at 150°C for about 10 minutes, until crispy. Remove from the oven and brush with olive oil while they are still hot.

Store in an airtight container until required.

Sponge Biscuits

These can be made into the long thin shapes known as ladies finger biscuits.

4 egg yolks
75 g castor sugar
75 g all-purpose flour, sieved
a few drops of vanilla essence
4 egg whites

Whisk the egg yolks and sugar until smooth. Fold in the sieved flour. Add the vanilla essence. Whisk the egg whites till they form hard peaks.

Line an oven tray with baking paper. Fold the egg whites into the egg yolk mixture and pipe onto the oven tray in the desired shape. Bake at 160°C for 10 minutes. Allow to cool on cooling wire. Store in an airtight container until you need them.

FOOD GLOSSARY

Aïoli
A Provençal emulsion of garlic, egg yolks, mustard and olive oil. Similar to mayonnaise.

Artichokes
A vegetable originating in Sicily — a very versatile vegetable with earthy flavours. Has an edible base and inedible central core (choke) and outer leaves. There are several varieties of artichoke.

Beurre blanc
Literally 'white butter', this is a classic French sauce made with white wine, shallots and butter.

Bouillabaisse
A Provençal seafood stew, made with an assortment of fish and seafood.

Button onions
Small pickling onions.

Capers
The unopened flower bud of the spiny Mediterranean shrub *Capparis spinosa*. The buds are dried and then salted or kept in vinegar. Rinse well before using.

Celeriac
A crunchy root vegetable from the celery family.

Ceviche
Raw fish marinated in lime juice until it takes on the texture of cooked fish.

Chantilly cream
Lightly sweetened whipped cream.

Chorizo
A spicy pork sausage made with chilli and other spices.

Ciabatta
A traditional Italian sourdough bread.

Crêpine
The lining of a pig's stomach. It is used to encase meats and fish like a sausage skin, to protect them from the heat and to keep all the flavours in.

Fritto misto
Literally Italian for mixed fried. Fritto misto refers to a selection of small pieces of fish, vegetables or meat, that are battered and then deep-fried.

Gnocchi
Small potato dumplings.

Gorgonzola
A cow's milk cheese with a blue vein running through it, from the Lombardy region of Italy.

Gravlax
(can also be spelt gravadlax)
Salmon that has been cured using salt and alcohol. The name comes from the Scandinavian words 'gravad' (buried) and 'lax' (salmon) — before refrigeration the salmon was cured by burying it underground throughout the cold Scandinavian winter.

Harissa paste
A very spicy North African chilli paste, which can be added to soups and sauces.

Jersey Bennes
New potatoes grown in Oamaru, South Island, New Zealand.

Mascarpone
A rich double-cream cheese, from Italy's Lombardy region. Can be mixed with savoury or sweet foods. Similar in texture to clotted cream.

Mesclun
Provençal word, from the verb 'to mix'. A mixture of different varieties of baby salad greens.

Paella
A Spanish rice dish made with saffron and a variety of fish and meats.

Pancetta

Pork belly cured for a few weeks and then air-dried for 6–8 months.

Pannacotta

Literally 'cooked cream' in Italian, pannacotta is a light dessert with a smooth jelly-like texture.

Paua

Also known as abalone. The edible part of this shellfish is the black muscle.

Pecorino

A ewe's milk cheese from Italy, soft in texture but quite tangy. Can be eaten fresh or when matured — maturation intensifies the flavour. Like parmesan it is traditionally used as an accompaniment to dishes.

Polenta

Italian food made from cornmeal, usually served with meat or fish. Can be served creamy or left to solidify, then sliced and sautéed, grilled or fried.

Porcini

A pungent and aromatic Italian mushroom. Available fresh during the damp autumn months. Dried porcini are readily available and have a more intense flavour. Soak dried porcini in a little warm water to reconstitute before using.

Prosciutto

Italian-style cured ham.

Remoulade

A traditional French sauce made from mayonnaise and mustard.

Ricotta

A soft, fresh curd cheese.

Rocket

An aromatic green salad leaf, also known as arugula. Can be eaten raw or cooked.

Roma tomato

A flavourful egg-shaped tomato, also called 'plum tomato'.

Romesco sauce

A spicy Spanish sauce of red capsicums, chillies and garlic, with roasted almonds.

Rouille

A spicy Provençal mayonnaise made with chillies, red capsicum and garlic. A traditional accompaniment to fish stews such as bouillabaisse.

Saffron

More expensive than gold, saffron is the dried red stigma from the crocus flower and is grown mainly in Spain and Turkey.

Salsa rosso

A chunky red salsa made from roasted red capsicums, basil, garlic, tomatoes and olive oil.

Salsa verde

A smooth green salsa, made from mixed green herbs and anchovies.

Tapenade

A thick Provençal sauce made from olives, olive oil, lemon juice and anchovies.

Tart tatin

A French upside-down tart. Traditionally made with apple.

Tzatziki

A refreshing Greek dip made from cucumber and yoghurt, flavoured with mint, garlic and olive oil.

Velouté

A stock-based white sauce.

Zibibbo

A grape variety grown on the Italian island of Pantelleria and used to make dessert wine.

GLOSSARY OF COOKING TERMS

Blind baking
Lining a mould with pastry, then lining the pastry with greaseproof paper, filling this with lima or haricot beans, then baking. This cooks the pastry before the filling is added.

Confit
A method of slow cooking in fat.

En croûte
Encased in pastry.

En papillote
Cooking inside a paper bag. The food steams as it bakes inside the paper. Traditionally used as a cooking method for fish.

Escalope
The French term for a very thin slice of meat or fish.

Julienne
Matchstick-thin strips.

Rillette
A method of cooking meat or fish resulting in a coarse-textured pâté.

Sauté
Frying food quickly in a small amount of oil.

Sweating
Frying vegetables in a little fat over low heat to soften without colouring.

MEASUREMENTS FOR THE COOK

All of the recipes in this book have been made using metric measurements. Using cup measurements is not as accurate as using a metric scale. I would highly recommend purchasing one to achieve perfect results.

1 teaspoon	5 ml
1 tablespoon	1 ml
½ cup	125 ml
1 cup	250 ml
4 cups	1 litre
1 pint	625 ml (2½ cups)
1 oz	30 g
6 oz (1 lb)	450 g
2¼ lb	1 kg

OVEN TEMPERATURES

All the recipes were tested and made in the kitchen at Zibibbo using a convection oven. If your oven is like mine it has a mind of its own and only you will know its secrets. The temperatures will vary according to brand and size. Also, like anything, practice makes perfect.

Very cool	130°C	250°F
Cool	150°C	300°F
Warm	170°C	325°F
Medium	180°C	350°F
Medium-hot	190–200°C	375–400°F
Hot	220°C	425°F
Very hot	230–250°C	475°F

SOURCES AND RESOURCES

These are the suppliers I use to make the wheel of fortune at Zibibbo keep on working. When you find your own suppliers build up a relationship with them and let them know what you like and may want from time to time. Sometimes chopping and changing suppliers will not get their loyalty.

3 Terraces Vineyard
Daikins Road
East Taratahi, Wairarapa
Ph: 0064 6 372 3355

AngusPure Beef
109 Shriffs Road
Palmerston North
Ph: 0064 4 353 6683
Supplier of Aged Angus beef.
The only brand of beef used at Zibibbo.

Cook Strait Seafoods
8–21 Lorne Street
Wellington
Ph: 0064 4 383 3933
Suppliers of seafood and shellfish.

La Bella Italia
10 Nevis Street
Petone, Wellington
Ph: 0064 4 566 9303
Email: ciao@labellaitalia.co.nz

Le Panto
11 Wentworth Street
Wellington
Email: sales@lepanto.co.nz
Web: www.lepanto.co.nz
Le Panto is a family-run business that specialises in Greek products.

Mediterranean Food Warehouse
42 Constable St, Newtown
Wellington
Ph: 0064 4 939 8100
Email: medifoods@paradise.co.nz
Web: www.medifoods.co.nz
Supplier of specialist Italian products.

Mushroom City
271 College Street
Palmerston North
Ph: 0064 6 358 4368
Suppliers of fresh wild mushrooms.

Pohangina Valley Venison
Reynard Farm
Pohangina Valley Road
RD 14, Ashhurst
Tel: 0064 6 326 9377
Fax: 0064 6 329 4788
Email: robinreynard@xtra.co.nz
Pohangina Valley Venison specialises in free-range New Zealand farmed venison.

The Homestore
Level 1, Capital on the Quay
250 Lambton Quay, Wellington
Ph: 0064 4 499 4469
Supplier of specialist kitchen equipment, and all crockery and sundries used in the book were provided by the Homestore.

High Country Salmon
Wairepo Arm
Twizel
Ph: 021 400 383

INDEX